A Primer
on Natural
Resource
Science

A Primer on

Natural Resource Science

Fred S. Guthery

Texas A&M
University Press
College Station

Library of Congress Cataloging-in-Publication Data

Guthery, Fred S.

A primer on natural resource science / Fred S. Guthery. — 1st ed.

p. cm.

Includes bibliographical references and index.

ISBN-13: 978-1-60344-024-0 (cloth : alk. paper)

ISBN-10: 1-60344-024-0 (cloth : alk. paper)

ISBN-13: 978-1-60344-025-7 (pbk. : alk. paper)

ISBN-10: 1-60344-025-9 (pbk. : alk. paper)

1. Science—Methodology. 2. Natural resources—Management—Research. I. Title.

Q175.G865 2008

507.2—dc22

2007037646

To graduate students
in the natural resource sciences.
We graybeards owe you much.
You keep our minds fresh,
you inspire us with your progress,
and you do most of the work.

Contents

Preface

My introduction to the philosophy of science occurred in 1987 when I was charged with teaching a graduate course in wildlife research methods; the course was to include lectures on the philosophy of science. I realized then that I was a Ph.D. with 17 years of wildlife research experience, and I had not been exposed (nor had I exposed myself) to philosophy-of-science issues. Preparation of those lecture notes piqued my interest in the broader aspects of science, or the nature of science, as it applies specifically to field ecology. The nature of science includes the philosophy but goes beyond into realms of sociality, creativity, practice, methodology, and logic.

I imagine that current graduate students in the natural resource sciences receive minimal exposure to the nature of science. This lack of exposure reduces the rate at which sound knowledge accumulates. Students have little or no idea what a research hypothesis is, but they are likely overexposed to the now-infamous null hypothesis, which I argue is one form of nonscientific hypothesis. Induction? Retroduction? Deduction? The hypothetico-deductive method? These processes are never or rarely addressed in graduate curricula. Nor are graduate students taught that their greatest hindrance as budding scientists is their speciation; evolution has dealt them severe handicaps they had better know about and deal with if they want to leave better approximations of truth in their theses, dissertations, and career legacies. These same evolutionary handicaps also suppress scientific creativity. Creativity is thought to be a strong correlate of the rate at which knowledge grows in a discipline.

Graduate students receive training, possibly extensive, in data analysis tools such as statistics and model selection. However, they receive no training on the roles of these tools in the grand panorama of science, in part because practicing statisticians, though a species of scientist, seldom know how natural resource science works. Nor do these statisticians apprehend the clamor of nature, and they cannot put the proper perspectives on the rote procedures they teach. Graduate students need to know the role of statistics in natural resource science; it is a minor tool that does not eliminate the need for human judgment.

The first part of this book I have classified under the heading "Perspectives." It starts with a discussion of the nature of science with a focus on natural resource science, and it explicitly or implicitly introduces the remaining topics in the book. Chapter topics include types of hypotheses, reasoning (induction, deduction, retroduction), the nature of facts, physiological and social shortcomings of humans as scientists, methods of increasing creativity, and critical thinking. The objective of the first part is to provide an overview of the cultural, logical, and inspirational aspects of natural resource science.

I have classified topics in the second part of the book under the heading "Practice." These topics include observational versus experimental science; the role of mathematics; the role, misuses, and danger of statistics; model selection; and model interpretation. When discussing statistical issues, I focus on "what they don't tell you in class." The topics in the second part also include a discussion of means versus ends in natural resource science; humankind has a tendency to exalt means (methods) at the expense of ends (growing knowledge). Also, exaltation of means results in mandated behaviors, most of which do not cut across all of science. I conclude with a chapter on publishing your results, a mandate that does cut across all of science. The objective of the second part is to provide an overview, warts and all, of the more or less mechanical parts of science.

I aimed this primer at graduate students (M.S., Ph.D.) in wildlife science and other natural resource sciences, but I believe it will be useful for more mature scientists as well. The primer is comprehensive in that it introduces several key concepts in science. However, it is not comprehensive in that books have been written on each of the concepts I introduce. In essence, I have reduced that knowledge to lengthy abstracts. I hope students of natural resource science will delve more deeply into these topics, as their conscience dictates.

I end each chapter with a perspectives section. The purpose of this section is to accent key topics in the chapter and put them in context relative to a larger view of science than the chapter covers. I will try to refrain from using the word *should* in the perspectives because, as Petr Skrabanek (1940–94) observed about the practice of medical science, "It is essential to keep 'what is' separate from 'what ought to be.'" "What is" is dispassionate; "what ought to be" is human value.

Acknowledgments

R. Dwayne Elmore, James H. Shaw, Markus J. Peterson, and Eric C. Hellgren kindly reviewed the entire manuscript in draft form. Bret Collier and Ralph L. Bingham reviewed selected chapters. Thank you for your lucid critiques.

The material in some chapters was developed for refereed articles in collaboration with colleagues. For contributions here, I thank Markus J. Peterson, Jeffrey J. Lusk, Leonard A. Brennan, and Ralph L. Bingham.

Perspectives

CHAPTER 1

The Nature of Science

Science is a lie detector.
—Brian L. Silver (1998:20)

Science . . . is the organized, systematic enterprise that gathers knowledge about the world and condenses the knowledge with testable laws and principles.
—Edward O. Wilson (1998:53; emphasis in original)

The central aim of science is to render the complexities of the universe transparent, so that we can see through them to the simplicities beneath.
—Jack Cohen and Ian Stewart (1994:29)

Science ranges across a vast panorama of endeavor. At one extreme of the range, we have detailed description, generally associated with atomization of subject matter (reductionism): particle physics, chemistry, molecular genetics, cell biology. At the other extreme we have the study of small to large systems: Newtonian mechanics, thermodynamics, natural selection, cosmology. The reductionists work with parts; the systematists with the expression of emergent properties and underlying principles of interacting parts. Thus, science as a body of tasks ranges from micro description to macro generalization and includes all possible levels of detail and grand sweep between these bounds.

Despite the diversity of scientific enterprise, there are common themes in all of science. These include underlying assumptions and philosophies as well as the normal activities of scientists. The activities include description of phenomena, pattern finding, hypothesis formulation, hypothesis testing, theory development, and methods development and testing. Of course, the greatest common denominator across science is thinking. Use of the mind alone leads to the discovery of great flaws in thinking and the production of great insight. This chapter introduces the common themes in science, including natural resource science.

Basic Assumptions and Philosophy

"In the methodology and the practice of science are many assumptions of value" (Houghton 1994:148). "For instance, that there is an objective world of value out there to discover, that there is value in the qualities of elegance and economy in scientific theory, that complete honesty and cooperation between scientists are essential to the scientific enterprise."

Houghton's statement reflects the philosophical infrastructure of science under modernism (a philosophy that arose in the eighteenth century and that implied reason and science rather than superstition and faith should be used to understand nature). The key assumption is that "there is an objective world of value out there." If the assumption holds, then there is objective truth out there and it is the quarry of scientists. However, the history of science teaches that accepted truth changes as explicit and implicit assumptions fail, accuracy of measurement improves, methodological bias becomes apparent, and knowledge expands. "The road to truth is always under construction; the going is the goal" (Berman 2000:138).

Postmodernists take a different view of scientific knowledge. They view knowledge as largely an outcome of zeitgeist (the spirit and values of the times) and the cultural affiliation of scientists (Gross and Levitt 1994). Based on that premise, they say scientific knowledge does not represent objective truth. Their arguments have some merit because human values (desires) and sociality hang like a pall over the accrual of objective knowledge.

Scientists, of course, must be aware of human shortcomings, especially their own, in the search for reliable knowledge. I will elaborate these ideas more fully in chapter 5. Scientists are, to a lesser or greater degree, subject to greed, vanity, egocentrism, and tribe allegiance. Human values and vested interest pollute the search for reliable knowledge. These foibles limit what scientists do perceive and even what they *can* perceive. The foibles lead inevitably to the formulation and propagation of false knowledge, which Romesburg (1981:293) defined as "false ideas that are mistaken for knowledge."

Based on the assumption of an objective reality available for discovery, the philosophers of science have done considerable reasoning on how to discover that reality. *Reasoning* is a key word here, for their ideas are perforce based on thought. They use formal logic to judge the relative merit of induction (generalizing from a specific event) and deduction (predicting a specific event from a generalization). We will discuss these topics more fully in chapter 3. Suffice it to say at this point that both induction and deduction are essential concepts in the practice of science.

Another assumption mentioned by Houghton (1994:148) is "that there is value in the qualities of . . . economy in scientific theories." The desirability of economy, or simplicity, is widely accepted among scientists. The idea owes to William of Ockham (or Occam), a fourteenth-century Franciscan, who wrote, "What can be explained by the assumption of fewer things is vainly explained by the assumption of more things" (Silver 1998:169). This principle has come to be known as Ockham's Razor, the principle of parsimony, or the principle of economy. The practical ramification of Ockham's Razor is that if you have a set of hypotheses that explain an event in nature equally well, the simplest hypothesis with respect to assumption tally is the best of the set (most likely to be true). Nowadays, hypotheses are said to be simpler if they entail fewer steps in a cause-effect chain, fewer parameters in a model, fewer assumptions, or, in general, fewer conditions to explain or predict.

As an example of the application of Ockham's Razor, consider the general observation that animals on a good nutritional plane tend to survive better and produce more young than animals on a poor nutritional plane. Now consider the fact that northern bobwhites (*Colinus virginianus*) tend to be poor survivors and good producers in northern latitudes, whereas they tend to be good survivors and poor producers in southern latitudes (Guthery 1997; Guthery et al. 2000). To explain the latter observation in terms of nutrition, we would have to hypothesize that summer foods are more nutritious and winter foods less nutritious in northern latitudes, whereas winter foods are more nutritious and summer foods less nutritious in southern latitudes. We might pit these hypotheses against the observation that winters are relatively severe in northern latitudes, whereas summers are relatively severe in southern latitudes. A weather hypothesis for explaining latitudinal patterns in bobwhite demography is simpler than the nutrition hypothesis and therefore takes precedence under Ockham's Razor.

Statistical modeling of the relation between dependent and independent variables provides another application of the principle of parsimony. Suppose we have data on a variable y that is some function of a variable x. We have 3 competing models:

$$y = a + bx,$$
$$y = \exp(a + bx), \text{ and}$$
$$y = a + bx + cx^2.$$

The constants (a, b, c) in these models represent parameters that must be estimated. The first 2 models are equally parsimonious because each has 2 parameters, whereas the third model has 3 parameters. Thus, if each of these models explained a relationship equally well, the researcher would reject the third model (most complex) on the basis of parsimony. I will address model selection in greater detail in chapter 11.

Ockham's Razor is a useful principle for reasons of likelihood. On the one hand, the simplest hypothesis in a set of hypotheses may be the least likely to appear out of the blue, so it must be closer to the truth than the alternatives (Feynman 1998). Newton's inverse square law of gravitational attraction was regarded by Feynman as a concept so simple that it must be true. Diamond's (1997) conjecture that the cultural effects of crop domestication spread more easily along longitudinal than latitudinal gradients is singular in its simplicity. (This would occur because a domesticated plant may have a greater longitudinal than latitudinal range where it is adapted to prevailing climate.)

On the other hand, the simplest hypothesis may be the most likely to appear. "Facts" as we know them are problematic (chapter 4). Facts might have truth-values <1, implying they are not completely true (truth-value $= 1$). It follows that a longer chain of facts leading to an outcome would be expected to have lower truth-values than a shorter chain. Suppose the truth-value of a hypothesis is correlated with the product of truth-values in a chain of explanations. If all the facts in a chain of events had a truth-value of 0.9, then a 2-event chain would have a truth-value proportional to $0.9^2 = 0.81$, whereas a 5-event chain would have a truth-value proportional to $0.9^5 = 0.59$. The shorter chain (2 events) is more likely than the longer chain (5 events). For this reason, molecular taxonomists rely on the most parsimonious evolutionary tree (the one with the smallest number of changes) to explain relationships between and among taxonomic units (Avise 1994:122).

Bear in mind, however, that application of Ockham's Razor represents failure, for knowing truth, a scientist would not have to invoke a mildly metaphysical standard of judgment. Indeed, perhaps the razor should be called Ockham's Crutch. Oreskes et al. (1994:645) argued that

> Ockham's razor is perhaps the most widely accepted example of an extraevidential consideration [in model selection]. Many scientists accept and apply the principle in their work, even though it is an entirely metaphysical assumption. There

is scant empirical evidence that the world is actually simple or that simple accounts are more likely than complex ones to be true. Our commitment to simplicity is largely an inheritance of [fourteenth-century] theology.

I disagree with Oreskes et al. to a degree because, as I argued above, there are logical reasons to expect simpler is better, given some universe of discourse. However, the simplest hypothesis or model is not necessarily the best hypothesis or model. Ockham's Razor probably becomes less useful as the complexity of a research topic increases. "Nowhere is [Ockham's] Razor more misplaced," for example, "than in a science of culture" (Plotkin 2000:80). Ecosystems, like cultures, are complex, so the natural resource scientist should regard Ockham's Razor as, at best, a prosthesis for amputated scientific endeavor. The natural resource scientist must *judge* both the complexity and power of hypotheses when accepting or rejecting competing alternatives.

Major Activities of Scientists
Description
All forms of science have descriptive underpinnings, and natural resource science is no exception. Description is based on motive—desire to know—rather than hypothesis. Description is essential because it is impossible to conduct other processes of science (e.g., hypothesis formulation) without a bank of descriptive data. Ideas do not spontaneously appear without observations; for example, try thinking of something about nothing.

In natural resource science, descriptive studies (natural history) address topics such as diet, reproduction (e.g., clutch size, litter size), behavior, habitat use, mobility and ranges, and so on. Natural history originally meant natural description (Schmidly 2005). The results of natural history research could be viewed as the mathematical logic of field biology in that the facts gathered probably are as pure as any facts in field biology. Descriptive data are necessary fodder for thought, and they may yield insight and original research questions.

For example, my research team recently obtained descriptive data on temperature dynamics in bobwhite nests (Guthery, Ryback, et al. 2005). Temperatures showed considerable variation, and the average temperature was well below that recommended for artificial incubation, which takes place at a constant temperature. We wondered whether there might be some fitness benefit associated with variable egg temperatures, and whether temperature variation might be associated with higher hatching rates in artificial incubators. The point is that the descriptive results generated the questions.

The estimation of magnitudes of effects is a form of descriptive science. Effect estimation is appropriate when a relationship is known or a treatment has known effects but the strength of the relationship or the size of an effect is in question. This type of simple descriptive study is common in natural resource science, although it often is camouflaged with mundane hypotheses, gratuitous predictions, and statistical folderol.

For example, there is no doubt that protein is an essential nutrient for reproduction in wild animals. Thus, a study of protein effects on reproduction provides yet another estimate of the degree to which different protein levels affect a reproduction variable. Likewise, many relationships are known to exist in nature and need not be tested per se. The strength (magnitude) of a relationship might be in question. Studies of the response of wildlife individuals or populations to management treatments are often an exercise in estimating the magnitudes of effects. It is somewhat silly to suppose researchers would test a treatment if they expected it to have no effect.

Descriptive results serve additional purposes in science. Collections of descriptive data are indispensable because they may lead to the discovery of patterns (trends or recurrences). The patterns discovered, or the descriptive data per se, might lead to explanations (how) or hypotheses on cause (why).

Pattern Finding

When several bodies of descriptive data have accumulated, the natural resource scientist is positioned to search for prevailing patterns in the knowledge base (synthesize). How does one search for patterns in published research? Obviously, one has to become cognizant of the relevant information (i.e., study it) that has accumulated on some topic, abstract saliencies from that information, and discern patterns, if possible. Constructing maps, figures, or tables from existing results may facilitate insight.

A classic example of pattern finding in the annals of science involves the periodic table of the elements (Bronowski 1973:322–26). Dmitri Ivanovich Mendeleev, a Russian chemist, wrote the names and atomic weights of elements on note cards and laid out the cards according to patterns of atomic weights. This revealed families of ele-

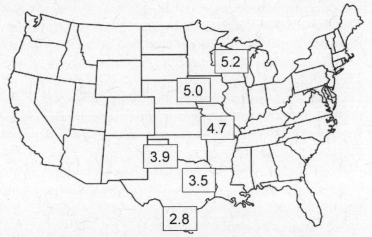

Fig. 1-1 Latitudinal trends in autumn age ratios (juveniles/adult) in midcontinent populations of northern bobwhites. The graphic shows a pattern (latitudinal gradient) in production and, by inference, survival rates.

ments with similar chemical properties. Mendeleev had the presence of mind to recognize gaps in the data—chemical elements that would later be discovered.

As a personal example of pattern finding, I came to recognize from the descriptive literature that age ratios of northern bobwhites were higher in northern latitudes and lower in southern latitudes. I constructed a graphic to illustrate this aspect of bobwhite demography (Guthery 2000; Fig. 1-1). The mere act of plotting age ratios at the approximate locations where samples were collected revealed a remarkable association (pattern) between latitude and productivity. Because, under mild assumption, average annual age ratios contain information on annual mortality rates (the percentage of juveniles reflects the annual mortality rate in populations with known trends), the graphic simultaneously revealed an association between latitude and annual mortality rates. The simple geographic pattern had broad implications on theories of bobwhite demography and harvest management (Guthery et al. 2000).

Hypothesis Formulation

"The classical procedure in science is to formulate a hypothesis and then carry out an experiment that is capable of disproving it" (Alexander 1996:146). We will see in the next chapter that the word *hypoth-*

esis has different meanings in science. At this point, we can define hypothesis as a tentative explanation for something; the explanation serves as the basis for further research.

Why should we be concerned that an experiment can disprove a hypothesis? Because if a hypothesis or theory conceivably can be disproved by observation or experiment, if it is testable, then it might well belong in the realm of science. Testability (falsifiability) is Popper's (1959:78) criterion of demarcation between scientific and nonscientific hypotheses. If not testable, a hypothesis might belong in the realm of faith or metaphysics (attempts to understand nature with pure reason). As we shall see in chapter 2, however, untestable hypotheses can be useful in science.

As with any principle or protocol of science, the criterion of testability should not be accepted blindly. "Popper's criterion . . . does demarcate between empirical [based on measurement or observation] and metaphysical statements," observes Skrabanek (2000:116), "but it is so wide that it allows non-metaphysical nonsense to slip in." For example, early Europeans thought children with Down syndrome occurred when a human being mated with a werewolf (*Canis quirkii;* Lopez 2004). Surely this hypothesis is testable with molecular genetics analysis, but just as surely it is nonsense. Finally, some theorems of mathematics such as Bernoulli's Law of Large Numbers cannot be tested, but we judge them scientific. (Bernoulli's Law states, approximately, that if the probability of an event is p, the relative frequency of the event will approach p in repeated independent trials as the number of trials approaches huge numbers.)

Moreover, sometimes we are less interested in a claim's testability than its heuristic value (Sorenson 1992:97), in which case testability is not especially germane. A claim has heuristic value (encourages discovery) if it leads to original thinking and alternative hypotheses. For example, Gause's Competitive Exclusion Principle is not testable (Sinclair 1991) but it is a metaphysical springboard for further thought on ecological competition. Indeed, twenty-first-century science is a blend of metaphysics and empiricism (Seager 2000).

At a minimum, the formulation of a testable hypothesis entails the availability of observations in need of explanation. The scientist then conjectures on whether a phenomenon exists, how it can be explained, or why it came to pass. Hypothesis formulation is, accordingly, a matter of pure thought as influenced by the ideas held in a mind.

Hypothesis Testing

Some forms of legitimate natural resource science do not entail hypothesis testing (Guthery, Lusk, et al. 2004). Natural history and estimation of magnitudes of effects are examples. In the former case the acquisition of descriptive information justifies the study, and in the latter case an effect or relationship is already known based on existing knowledge.

Hypothetico-deductive (H-D) experimentation is the classical method of testing a hypothesis. It involves formulating a hypothesis and deducing events that will be observed under experimentation if the hypothesis is true: "If my conjecture on explanation or cause is true, then I expect to observe these outcomes in an experiment." For example, "If salmon (*Oncorhynchus* spp.) use olfaction to navigate to natal streams, then (I deduce) streams will have unique chemical signatures." Unique chemical signatures would be requisite for salmon to navigate to a specific stream by olfaction. If the deduction, or prediction, is observed, then the hypothesis is supported by experimental results. Otherwise, it is not supported. In application in field ecology, the H-D method has flaws that we will discuss in chapter 3.

A large body of statistical tools has been developed for testing null (no effect) hypotheses. These include significance testing based on test statistics such as t and F. These tools and others like them were developed because we encounter variability in research results, which leads to uncertainty. The variability might occur because we have imprecise measurements, incomplete knowledge of causes, and/or some combination of these and/or other factors. The statistical tools provide logical, mathematical methods of dealing with uncertainty en route to conclusions. A common property of all such tools is a direct or indirect basis in probability. Scientists, accordingly, may judge the merit of hypotheses (some say adjust their beliefs about a hypothesis) relative to whether the hypotheses are probable or improbable based on observation and analysis.

Rational scientists should view statistical tools as purveyors of evidence upon which to base *judgments*. All such tools are based on assumptions that might or might not be relevant in understanding nature; the null hypothesis is seriously flawed (chapter 10). No such tool can override the effects of poor experimental design, human bias, or idiosyncratic data (data that, for one reason or another, poorly reflect the state of nature at the time of data collection).

Theory Development

After a hypothesis has passed repeated and severe challenges, it may become a theory. "A theory is a good theory if it satisfies two requirements: It must accurately describe a large class of observations [patterns] on the basis of a model that contains only a few arbitrary elements [simplification], and it must make definite predictions about the results of future observations" (Hawking 1988:9). Theories abstract "what is regular and readily reproducible from reality and present it in idealized form, valid only under certain assumptions and boundary conditions" (Eigen and Winkler 1981:16). An important process of science is the hewing of simplicity from complexity through theory development (Atkins 1995:126), the compression of information on offer into simple models with explanatory or predictive power (Barrow 1995:47).

A few simple rules, the stuff of theory, may lead to extremely complex outcomes. As an analogy, Russell (2000) claims mathematics in all its complexity and intricacy arose from about 12 primitive notions. The chore of ecological scientists is to find the few primitive notions from which we can deduce all the clamor of nature. Darwin's theory of natural selection is an example of a powerful primitive notion that is relevant to ecology. There is no higher pinnacle in scientific achievement than to discover simple rules that explain complex behaviors.

Development and Testing of Methods and Techniques

Many papers in natural resource journals involve the development and testing of methods and techniques. Such work might involve an assessment of the merit of different estimators of a particular variable. For example, numerous papers have evaluated different estimators of home range size. New methods of estimating or analyzing different variables or situations continuously arise from the human mind; these, in turn, need to be assessed for strengths and weaknesses. When new technologies such as global positioning systems appear, their performance under field conditions needs to be evaluated. I view methods research as more technological than scientific. Nonetheless, scientists need to understand the tools they apply. As methods research leads to improved measurement of variables, this, in turn, leads to improved reliability of the knowledge gained from measurement.

The Role of Mind

Scientific knowledge is, above all else, a product of the human mind. It has the ability to ask innocent questions with catastrophic answers, to recognize patterns and synthesize, to imagine things that do not really exist but that help us understand, and to speculate on explanations or causes based on the repository of knowledge available at the time. Too often scientists let the trappings of science—experimental design, statistical testing, model selection—take precedence over the application of good old-fashioned thought. There is a natural human tendency to confuse means (e.g., statistical tests) with ends (e.g., reliable knowledge), and that tendency is well illustrated in natural resource science (chapter 14).

In the philosophy of science, there have been two opposing views on how knowledge comes to be. Rationalism is the theory that the intellect is the true source of knowledge, whereas empiricism is the theory that sensory experience is the only source of knowledge. The practicing scientist must blend these theories to generate useful new knowledge. That is, the scientist must develop thoughts about phenomena (rationalism) and put those thoughts to experimental or observational test (empiricism).

Perspectives

This chapter is a bare-bones introduction to the nature of science, about which tomes have been written. Nonetheless, it raises important issues. The student of natural resource science should take note that 2 supposed canons of science—Popper's criterion of demarcation and Ockham's Razor—are incomplete if not imperfect. Yet the student will find that many members of the scientific community hold them in high esteem if not awe; the concepts are part of the religion of science. The phrase "testable hypothesis," for example, has become a shibboleth (a password that allows your entrance into the culture). Excepting honesty and integrity, there probably are few protocols of science that cut unconditionally across the practice. We will see additional much-revered though somewhat bastard standards and principles as the book unfolds.

Chapter 1 also sets up several of the topics that follow. In particular, the chapter introduces both hypothesis formulation as an important activity of scientists and the different types of hypotheses that may be formulated.

CHAPTER 2 Hypotheses

We shall . . . see that there are several kinds of hypotheses; that some are verifiable, and when once confirmed by experiment become truths of great fertility; that others may be useful to us in fixing our ideas; and finally, that others are hypotheses only in appearance.
—Henri Poincaré (1952:xxii)

The hypothesis is the principal intellectual instrument in research.
—W. I. B. Beveridge (1957:71)

There isn't a scientific method. There are many—and none of them is foolproof.
—Brian L. Silver (1998:23; emphasis in original)

Scientists widely regard hypotheses as key elements of science; indeed, most would say hypotheses are central. A hypothesis is generally viewed as a speculative thought, especially one that might explain something and is worthy of further investigation. Words such as *guess, conjecture, supposition, surmise,* and *speculation* are approximate synonyms in the proper context.

However, the word *hypothesis* has richer and deeper meanings in science than conveyed in the preceding paragraph. It often is accompanied by modifiers such as *nonscientific* or *research.* Each of these modified forms has subcategories. What I call a Poincaré hypothesis is an elegant mental construct, an unobservable, that scientists posit to explain or understand phenomena. This chapter defines and gives examples of the many types of hypotheses used in natural resource science.

Nonscientific Hypotheses

There are at least 3 kinds of nonscientific hypotheses. The first kind is a hypothesis that is always false. Although it seems weird that scientists would advance hypotheses that are always false, the practice is common. The statistical null hypothesis, widely applied in scientific research, is a priori false, in general. This will be explained in chapter 10.

The second kind of nonscientific hypothesis is one that is vacuously true (tautological, or necessarily true). Consider these examples:

* "Our objective was to test the hypothesis that blackbirds [Icteridae] select roosting locations according to specific habitat features" (Lyon and Caccamise 1981:435).

* "We tested the hypothesis that habitat characteristics differed among summer communal, winter communal, summer solitary, and winter solitary roosts. We also tested the hypothesis that roost habitat differed from habitat available at random" (Buehler et al. 1991).

* "We hypothesized that ocelots [*Leopardus pardalis*] would prefer large patches of closed canopy habitat [i.e., known preferred habitat] and avoid large patches of unsuitable habitat" (Jackson et al. 2005).

* "We hypothesized that occupied habitat would differ from a random sampling of available . . . habitat" (Patten et al. 2005).

* "Our hypothesis was that the mix of species in native seed mixes would establish as well as the mix of species in predominantly introduced species mixes, but that higher total seeding rates are necessary for them to do so" (Thompson et al. 2006:238). This hypothesis is vacuously true because native species have lower establishment rates than introduced species. If you plant native species at higher seeding rates, eventually establishment rates will equalize.

These hypotheses are simply assertions of the obvious. Vacuous hypotheses often indicate simple descriptive studies camouflaged as hypothesis-driven studies. They probably also imply cultural influence in that practitioners suppose in a tribal manner, and so do referees of articles, that it is good to state a hypothesis. Honesty and simplicity would be better served in natural resource science if researchers doing descriptive work simply listed their objectives. Here are some examples of objectives in descriptive studies:

* "The objective of our study was to determine the settlement patterns of offspring in this [red squirrel (*Tamiasciurus hudsonicus*)] population, and their fates" (Larsen and Boutin 1994:215).

* "The objectives of this study were to examine seasonal habitat use and home range size of gray partridge [*Perdix perdix*] in eastern South Dakota" (Smith et al. 1982:580).

* "The present study . . . was designed to investigate the energy economy of the Canada goose [*Branta canadensis*] in relation to variations in temperature and photoperiod to which it is

subjected during its annual cycle" (Williams and Kendeigh 1982:588).

* "This paper describes mobility, home range, and habitat use by mallard [*Anas platyrhynchos*] broods" (Talent et al. 1982:629).

The third kind of nonscientific hypothesis is one that is not testable (not falsifiable), as pointed out in chapter 1, and has no heuristic value. Generally, religious beliefs are not testable in a scientific sense. Here are some examples:

* My totem protects me from evil spirits.
* Souls are reincarnated in different life-forms.
* The diversity and complexity of life are a product of intelligent design.

Nonfalsifiable hypotheses need not, however, be based on religious belief.

Scientific Hypotheses
Not Testable

In the first chapter I mentioned Gause's Principle of Competitive Exclusion as a scientific hypothesis that is not testable (Sinclair 1991:767): "No two species can live in the same niche, and if they attempt to do so one will exclude the other through competition." Sinclair notes that the principle is not testable because it is not reasonable to suppose a scientist could ever determine whether two species have the same niche.

Another example of a nonfalsifiable yet scientific hypothesis is the thrifty gene hypothesis (O'Keefe and Cordain 2004). It asserts that because human beings evolved in a variable environment, they developed the physiological ability to rapidly store excess energy intake in the form of fat, which would provide energy for lean times. This hypothesis could not be tested with humans because it would involve controlled environments in evolutionary time scales starting with experimental subjects lacking the physiological ability to rapidly store fats.

Although the Competitive Exclusion Principle and the thrifty gene hypothesis are not testable, they are reasonable subjects of scientific discourse. That is, they have heuristic value. The Exclusion Principle places a conceptual limit (identical niches) on the question of competition. The gene hypothesis provides a conceptual background for the problem of obesity in twenty-first-century America. A lack of falsifiability in a hypothesis does not necessarily imply a lack of scientific value in the hypothesis.

Models

Mathematical and certain statistical models may be viewed as a form of hypothesis because they are conjectures on patterns or processes in nature (Guthery, Lusk, et al. 2004). In practice, though, statistical models tend to be descriptive in the sense that they estimate magnitudes of effects already known, for example, the strength of a relationship between two variables. It is also possible that competing statistical models could be used to test competing research hypotheses (defined later). The idea would be to advance the models as deductions, collect data, and determine which model best explained or described the data. Such use of statistical models is quite rare, however.

Poincaré Hypotheses

Scientists have long held that a hypothesis can be an assumption, something taken as true, or something *imagined* for the sake of argument or explanation. I call these Poincaré (1952) hypotheses because he devoted a book to this type of hypothesis, which Romesburg (1991) called an isolate and Feynman (1998) called a construct. The hypothesis as an imaginary construct is quite abstract and relatively rare in natural resource science at this time. Some examples of Poincaré hypotheses follow.

1. *The threshold of security* (Errington 1945). Errington observed, early in his research career, that northern bobwhites tended to a relatively constant spring density, regardless of the number in the fall population. He postulated the existence of a threshold of security to explain similar breeding densities given variable fall densities. Birds in excess of the threshold, he surmised, are more vulnerable to loss, whereas birds below the threshold experience little loss. The threshold is imaginary, though it might be considered a homologue of carrying capacity. The threshold concept is now regarded as false, but it is a good example of hypothesis as an imaginary construct.

2. *The niche as an* n-*dimensional hypervolume* (Hutchinson 1957). Niche itself is an imaginary phenomenon referring to the

role or function of an organism within a population or community. Viewed as an *n*-dimensional hypervolume, the niche has *n* dimensions, which might include places in a food web, competitive interactions, abiotic requirements, and so on. Hypervolume simply means the niche has >3 dimensions. Hutchinson's view of niche provides a construct for understanding partitioning of resources among sympatric organisms.

3. *Slack in configuration of habitat patches* (Guthery 1999b). Slack is a conceptual property associated with the configuration (arrangement, amount) of habitat objects such as woody and herbaceous cover. Slack implies that many different arrangements might be optimal for an organism. When slack exists, we deduce that animals behave independently of constructs such as edge and diversity, among others.

Research Hypotheses

Research hypotheses address questions of whether (existence), how (explanation), or why (cause). These types of research hypotheses are the workhorses of hypothesis-driven natural resource science; they serve as the basis for hypothesis testing through deduction, which we address in chapter 3.

Existential (whether) hypotheses are conjectures on the existence of some circumstance, pattern, or phenomenon. Following are some examples of existential hypotheses:

* Birds forage more efficiently in flocks than as individuals (Hilborn and Mangel 1997:25).

* Within the northern hemisphere, clutch size for a bird species is larger in northern than in southern latitudes (Ashmole's hypothesis).

* Biological objects are randomly dispersed on an area.

* These treatments have no effect on a response variable of interest (null hypothesis; an effect either does or does not exist).

* Larger home ranges are associated with lower survival in fox squirrels (*Sciurus niger*) (Conner 2001).

* "We hypothesize that altered immunocompetence is a primary physiological mechanism by which environment

regulates survival and ultimately the dynamics of small mammal populations" (Lochmiller et al. 1994:237).

* Animals and autistic people perceive a world of fine detail, whereas normal people perceive impressions filtered from fine detail (Grandin and Johnson 2004).

The second form of research hypothesis is a conjecture on how some event came to pass, not whether or why, and it results in an explanation. "How" questions ask in what manner or by what means or process. For example, a question that has long intrigued biologists is, How do migratory animals navigate? Some explanations that have been put forth (how) are an ability to sense Earth's magnetic fields or an ability to use celestial navigation. In the case of migratory fish such as salmon, an explanation is olfaction (recognizes odors of natal stream).

The third form of research hypothesis is a question of why but not how or whether. "Why" questions ask for what purpose, reason, or cause; with what intention, justification, or motive: Why did this event occur? What caused this event? These hypotheses are examples based on "why" questions:

* Snowshoe hare (*Lepus americanus*) populations begin cyclic declines in abundance because of winter food shortages (Vaughan and Keith 1981).

* Birds cache seeds on south slopes instead of north slopes because south slopes are more likely to remain snow free during winter (Romesburg 1981).

* "[I]t is possible that individuals [Townsend's voles (*Microtus townsendii*)] disperse or delay sexual maturation in response to severe competition and that further dispersal takes place if any remaining individual is at risk of inbreeding" (Lambin 1994:225). This statement may be rearranged to read, Townsend's voles disperse or delay sexual maturation because of severe competition; further dispersal occurs because of risk of inbreeding.

* People do not apply research results because they view research results as opinions.

* The harvest of trophy bucks leads to smaller antlers in deer populations because of genetic selection against trophy bucks

and for smaller bucks (more likely to survive hunting season and reproduce).

Note that the word *because* appears in each of the above examples of "why" hypotheses. This phrase implies that a cause has been proffered, but scientists have to be careful about ascribing causes. David Hume (1711–76) observed that, in the realm of experience, the only thing scientists can observe is a repeated conjunction between events and ascribe cause accordingly (Newton-Smith 2000). This means that a circumstance precedes an event in time or space, so the circumstance could be presumed a cause of the event. This notion of cause probably prevails among natural resource scientists. Hume believed, however, we have no legitimate idea of causation (necessity) that goes beyond observing conjoined events. If he is correct, then we cannot determine cause.

Subsequently, philosophers devised a means of working necessity into ascription of cause (Humphreys 2000:35): "We . . . have that event A caused event B if and only if (1) A occurred; (2) B occurred; and (3) the counterfactual 'If A had not occurred, [then] B would not have occurred is true (or can be asserted).'" In a practical sense, there may be no way of knowing whether event B would not have occurred absent event A.

There are further problems in determining cause. Consider the hypothesis that snowshoe hare populations begin cyclic declines in abundance because of winter food shortages (Vaughan and Keith 1981). A legitimate follow-up question is, What causes winter food shortages? We could go on: What causes the cause of winter food shortages? Such reasoning might take us back to the Big Bang, which could be construed as the cause of everything except itself. Because of a high degree of arbitrariness in ascribing cause, as the hare hypothesis illustrates, some scientific disciplines have trended away from "why" hypotheses to "how" hypotheses (Beveridge 1957:126).

Another problem with the concept of cause in field ecology is that an outcome might be a product of several explanatory causes. For example, a change in a wildlife community after a perturbation such as timber harvest may be explainable on the basis of changes in the structure or composition of plant communities, quantity of food supplies, or microclimate; changes in the community itself that invoke further change; and other factors that may act uniquely or in concert on the postperturbation community. One can only list and contemplate possible causes in the presence of multiple and often interacting causes.

Natural resource scientists frequently receive criticism for confusing correlation and cause (e.g., Eberhardt 1970; Johnson 2002). Indeed, a dogmatic, oft-repeated principle is that "correlation does not imply cause and effect." The principle is but partially true; the implications of correlation are deeper than the principle admits.

There are at least 5 reasons why 2 variables (x, y) may be correlated (Campbell 1974):

1. Because x is the cause of y. Example: Among years, the effort expended by public hunters (hunter-days; y) increases with the abundance of game (x). The variables are correlated, and one could construe loosely that increases in game abundance cause increases in hunter effort.

2. Because y is the cause of x.

3. Because x and y interact with each other. In this situation, x might sometimes be the cause of y, and y might sometimes be the cause of x. From the first example above, we have that abundance of game governs hunting effort. Greater hunting effort would be associated with higher license revenue, some of which might be invested in habitat development and management. Such investments might cause greater hunting effort to increase the abundance of game.

4. Because x and y were correlated by chance in a sample.

5. Because both x and y are effects of a third variable outside the analysis. This circumstance entails a situation where a variable z causes x and y. Suppose z is the quantity of rainfall during a growing season. Rainfall might cause high production of grass and forbs directly and high production by wildlife populations indirectly. Thus, primary production and wildlife production would be correlated, but the cause of both would be rainfall.

Notice that cause is explicit in the first 3 items, although the third raises the interesting issue of mutual causation. So a more general principle is that "correlation *might* or *might not* imply cause and effect."

Despite the dubiety of determining causes in natural resource science, it is convenient in discourse and prediction to talk of cause and effect as events that are conjoined in time or space. Such discourse is the essence of management. However, natural resource scientists need to keep in mind that such determination of cause is somewhat arbitrary, and it hides a plethora of complexity and detail.

Perspectives

The key points in this chapter for the student of natural resource science are these:

1. If you are doing a descriptive study, simply list the objectives of the research. For description that does not involve relationships, it is impossible to imagine a nontrivial hypothesis upon which to base a study.

2. Beware of the vacuous hypothesis, for it implies vacuity (emptiness of mind) on your part. Again, if you are doing description, simply list the objectives of your study rather than try to embellish with some lame hypothesis.

3. Recognize that abstract thoughts in the form of Poincaré hypotheses may be employed to understand and predict, and that such hypotheses take science into elegance.

4. Where appropriate, formulate research hypotheses that ask whether, how, or why, and proceed with research that addresses the hypotheses.

5. Realize that identifying the cause of something may be difficult, and that in discourse we tend to arbitrarily assign cause and effect to conjoined events.

The mental process of formulating hypotheses remains largely unexplored at this point in the book. The next chapter delves into inductive, deductive, and retroductive reasoning in hypothesis formulation and testing.

CHAPTER 3

Induction, Deduction, and Retroduction

Many, if not most, . . . graduate students do not even understand the differences between induction and deduction.
—H. Charles Romesburg (1981:311)

There is a tradition of opposition between adherents of induction and of deduction. In my view it would be just as sensible for the two ends of a worm to quarrel.
—Alfred North Whitehead (cited in Peirce 2000:1340)

[N]o body of observations can prove *the hypothesis true, because [inductive] hypotheses make predictions that go beyond any body of evidence that we may have accumulated at any point in time.*
—Harold I. Brown (2000:196; emphasis in original)

Nobody argues with the assertion that accumulation of reliable knowledge is the prime goal of science. Yet there is considerable difference of opinion among philosophers and practicing scientists on how to judge the reliability of knowledge gathered under different methods of reasoning (induction, deduction, and retroduction).

Romesburg's (1981) article on gaining reliable knowledge influenced the manner in which wildlife scientists perceive knowledge. He pointed out that induction (generalizing from specific results) is the workhorse of wildlife science. Indeed, induction is policy in our journals as illustrated by the "Management Implications" section. This section operates, to some degree, under the premise that the results of a specific study will hold in a more general spatial and temporal context than where and when the study took place. Romesburg also pointed out that H-D experimentation is underused in wildlife science. H-D experimentation involves positing a research hypothesis, deducing outcomes that will hold under the hypothesis, and testing to determine whether the outcomes appear in experiment. Romesburg (1981:295) pointed out that untested hypotheses have gained "credence and the status of laws through rhetoric, taste, authority, and verbal repetition." "The H-D method," he argued, "is a way of raising the reliability of . . . speculation and, hence, the overall reliability of our knowledge. It is not a cure-all."

Like all human enterprises, natural resource science is a culture whose members perceive proprieties and improprieties in conduct. The philosophers of science, who are grounded in formal logic and who tend to see physics as science (with deference to Charles Darwin), have laid down the proprieties. One is the notion that, philosophically, induction holds no claim whatsoever on truth (Howson 2000). Another is the notion that the H-D method, though imperfect, at least represents a logically supported approach to truth seeking. Accordingly, wildlife scientists have extolled H-D experimentation (Guthery, Lusk, et al. 2001; Guthery, Brennan, et al. 2005; Garton et al. 2005) since Romesburg's (1981) article. We now realize there may be a major disconnect between the thinking of philosophers and the realities of natural resource science.

This chapter introduces induction, deduction, and retroduction (after-the-fact explanations) as methods of reasoning about the truth of propositions that describe or explain nature. I provide definitions, examples, and philosophical and practical considerations regarding the methods of reasoning. I also explain and provide examples of the H-D method and point out that it may be flawed when applied to research problems in field ecology.

Induction
Definition
Induction is reasoning from particular facts or individual cases to a general conclusion or principle. Also, the general conclusion is called an induction. Aldo Leopold (1933) observed that animals of low mobility requiring ≥ 2 cover types tended to be associated with edges between required cover types. From this observation, he induced the principle of edge: the density of animals on an area is proportional to the sum of the edges of required cover types on the area.

Examples
Inductions appear frequently in the literature of natural resource science. They can be identified whenever authors extrapolate the results of a particular study to a general situation, as in these examples:

* "The results of this study indicate that [construction of earthen dikes across wetlands] provides predator access and decreases avian productivity by a factor of 1.5–3× that of undisturbed wetlands. Thus, the widespread construction of [earthen dikes] in small prairie wetlands will be detrimental to the waterfowl resource" (Peterson and Cooper 1987:246).

* "My results suggest that lead shot is available to feeding waterfowl for many years, and that exposure of waterfowl to

lead poisoning will likely occur for >3 years after the lead shot is curtailed" (Flint 1998:1099).

* Concerning three-toed woodpeckers (*Picoides tridactylus*), Pechacek and Kristin (2004:690) induced from their results, "Based on the average distance for food gathering, dead trees should not be removed within a 250-m circle from nests."

* "The relationship between rainfall and avian reproduction appears to be mediated by arthropod abundance" (Bolger et al. 2005:402). This induction was based on a 2-year study of 4 bird species, and arthropod abundance was the only potentially causative variable measured.

* "The results of this study indicate that bullfrog [*Rana catesbeiana*] and green frog [*R. clamitans*] larvae strongly interact, both within and between year classes, over density ranges encountered in natural populations" (Werner 1994:205).

Each of these examples illustrates the extrapolation of specific results to general situations.

Philosophical Considerations

Philosophers of science regard inductive knowledge as less trustworthy than deductive knowledge or, in the extreme, not as knowledge at all (Howson 2000). In the philosophical limit, inductive knowledge operates under the assumption that the future will be like the past. These philosophers also argue that a sampled instance (the source of an induction) does not necessarily tell us anything about the infinitude of not-sampled instances (the target of induction). One counterexample falsifies an induction. The latter argument has practical merit in natural resource science; for example, Leopold's inductively based principle of edge has been repeatedly disproved.

Induction may be especially hazardous when the generalization drawn from data takes the form of a model. Consider the inductive model generated by Rosenberg and Anthony (1993), which predicts the density (y, no./ha) of Townsend's chipmunks (*Tomias townsendii*) as a function of the density (x, no./ha) of large hard snags:

$$y = 2.8 + 0.7x.$$

Although this model was a good predictor, given the data, it was based on a sample size of 5 observations. Accordingly, the model per se is of little value until tested on independent data. The model might serve as a basis for a research hypothesis that the density of large hard snags governs the density of chipmunks; this hypothesis could be tested by perturbation experiments (altering snag density).

Despite the philosophical and empirical dangers of induction, the practicing scientist has no alternative but to induce with some abandon; science would collapse otherwise (H. Brown 2000:196), in part because, strictly speaking, we gain no new knowledge from deduction (Campbell 1974:137). This statement holds because a deduction is a derivation from existing knowledge.

Campbell (1974) pointed out that the quality of an induction varies. We have no problem inducing whether we have diabetes based on a 1-ml sample of our blood. We can accept an inductive estimate of a population mean under random and sufficient sampling. Likewise, ecologists accept the results of a well-designed field study with sufficient sampling as inductively applicable to a more general situation. Their knowledge of the natural history of organisms under study might reinforce their trust in the generality of particular results. In a practical sense, induction does not take place in an epistemic vacuum (an absence of germane knowledge). "Rather, generalizations are accepted as a result of judgments made by skilled individuals who reflect on the information and the alternatives that are available in their field of expertise" (H. Brown 2000:196). This is an important point in the philosophy of natural resource science; it has no homologue that I know of in formal logic.

On the contrary, natural resource scientists might distrust results from a poorly designed study with insufficient sampling. So there are implicit filters for how natural resource scientists deal with induction, the infinitude of not-sampled instances be damned. Portions of the "Discussion" section of many articles could be viewed as active filtering of inductions. These portions are comparisons of inductive findings of the present study with inductive findings from earlier studies. To the extent that inductive findings are replicable, credence in them grows, despite the philosophers' objections. To the extent that these findings are not replicable, acceptance is suspended until further research or unifying hypotheses clarify the situation. A unifying hypothesis explains and resolves contradictory results that have arisen.

A logical curiosity in field ecology is that inductions might be amenable to deductive analysis through thought experiment. Consider as an example the inductively derived migration corridors of waterfowl (Bellrose 1976). These corridors are based on generalizations to migratory populations from the locations of a sample of band returns. We could deduce the geographic locations of corridors for ducks with 2 inductive facts of natural history: ducks migrate, and ducks are associated with water. The Mississippi River might be thus deduced as a migration corridor, a deduction that would be amply borne out by band-return data. Here we have a deduction and an induction being the same species. I do not know whether deductive support for an induction strengthens the induction; such support might make an induction deductively plausible, at most. No wonder Whitehead likened induction and deduction to quarreling ends of the same worm (see epigraph).

Although induction as a form of knowledge accrual is criticized in natural resource science (Romesburg 1981; Guthery, Lusk, et al. 2001; Guthery, Brennan, et al. 2005), the researcher has to recognize that induction has a valid place in natural resource science. The findings of descriptive natural history are inductive, but surely we can trust them into the near future. In some cases, the purpose of a study is simply to measure the magnitude of some effect. If design and sampling are sufficient to estimate the magnitude, we probably can trust the inductive knowledge that accrues. Finally, inductive knowledge is necessary as a foundation for generating hypotheses amenable to deductive challenge. That is, one may deduce and test for the occurrence of events from an inductively discovered event or pattern. As Whitehead (2000:405) observed, "The theory of Induction is the despair of philosophy—and yet all our activities are based upon it."

Deduction
Definition

Deduction is reasoning from a principle or premise to a specific event (a prediction or deduction). Also, the prediction itself is called a deduction. If the density of animals on an area is proportional to the sum of the edges of required cover types on the area, then we deduce that density will decline with removal of edge and increase with addition of edge.

Examples

I found a good example of hypothesis formulation and deduction in the medical literature. "The Compression of Morbidity [ill health] hypothesis maintains that the age of onset of significant disability may be moved upward [older ages] more rapidly than life expectancy, thus compressing morbidity into a shorter period at the end of life" (Fries 1984:354). Fries argued that death from senescence should be expected at around age 85 years, plus or minus. Accordingly, it might be possible to increase average life expectancy by delaying morbidity, but it might not be possible to increase maximum life expectancy because the physiological system collapses at older ages. If the compression of morbidity hypothesis is reasonable, then certain predictions ensue:

* The difference in life expectancy between males (lower) and females (higher) in the United States will decrease (because both sexes will trend toward the physiological limit of maximum longevity and eventually males will catch up with females).

* The standard deviation of age at death after age 10 will decrease. That is, more people will be dying at the physiologically limiting age, thus reducing variability in age at death.

The predictions (deductions) formulated by Fries are simply the outcomes of thinking through the Compression of Morbidity hypothesis and identifying events that must occur if the hypothesis is true. The deductions can be tested with long-term records on age at death of humans.

Spears et al. (1993) did a study that further illustrates the H-D process. The event in need of explanation was inconsistencies in the technical literature on the optimum seral stage for northern bobwhites: some authors recommended lower seral stages, whereas others recommended higher stages. The Spears et al. research hypothesis was that the optimum seral stage for bobwhites varies inversely with site productivity (lower seral stage is optimum on more productive sites; higher seral stage is optimum on less productive sites). Spears et al. reasoned that there existed an optimum biomass of grasses for bobwhites and that the optimum would occur in different seral stages on sites of different productivity. They deduced (predicted) an interaction effect between bobwhite abundance and seral stage in sites of different productivity: abundance would decline with seral stage in sites of higher productivity and increase with seral stage on sites of lower productivity. They also deduced the existence of habitat commonalities, or habitat features such as exposure of bare ground that would be similar in different seral stages, depending on site productivity. Field results, though somewhat ambiguous, were consistent with the deductions. Therefore, results tended to support rather than refute the research hypothesis. The hypothesis of Spears et al. was unifying because it resolved contradictions in the technical literature.

Rave and Baldassarre (1991) provide another example of H-D science in a field setting. They tested competing hypotheses— temperature effects, diet—explaining lipid dynamics in wintering green-winged teal (*Anas crecca*). They deduced that if mass of lipid reserves varied inversely with winter severity, then the temperature hypothesis was better supported. Conversely, if carcass composition varied more with food composition than winter severity, then the diet hypothesis was better supported.

Barten et al. (2001:78) used a blend of existential hypotheses (as defined in chapter 2) to ascertain whether and to what degree forage acquisition and predation risk (competing research hypotheses) governed the field behavior of female caribou (*Rangifer tarandus*). Under the forage-acquisition hypothesis they deduced, among other predictions, that "forage abundance and quality would be greater at sites used by females with young than at sites used by females without young." Under the predation-risk hypothesis, they deduced, among other predictions, that "forage abundance and quality would be lower at sites used by females with young than at sites used by females without young." All of these predictions are testable in the practical as well as theoretical sense.

Philosophical Considerations

The homage paid to H-D experimentation as a revealer of truth seems to have roots in formal logic. There, a deduction from a true premise is by definition (and obviously) true. A true premise does not permit a false deduction (Bandyopadhyay and Bennett 2004) because a false deduction from a true premise is, by definition, impossible. Thus, in an analogous manner, one might presume that a deduction from a true research hypothesis is true. I suppose this is inarguable if a research hypothesis is comprehensively, as opposed to fractionally, true (the hypothesis identifies one of multiple causes). I also admit it is tempting to suppose that truth may be revealed accordingly, but conditions are much more higgledy-piggledy in ecosystems than in syllogisms. As illustrated below, the observation, or lack thereof, of a deduction in a field experiment might leave the researcher with doubt over the merit of a hypothesis.

There seems to be no way to test "how" or "why" hypotheses (chapter 2) except by testing deductions from those hypotheses. That is the supreme justification for H-D experimentation—that it permits testing of research hypotheses. I cannot imagine how a "how" or "why" hypothesis could be tested inductively; I conjecture such a test is impossible. Romesburg (1981) lamented the failure of wildlife scientists to test hypotheses, especially those developed after the fact to explain an observation (retroductions). This failure was, I believe, his main point for the community of natural resource scientists, and its annulment necessitates use of the H-D method.

Despite the apparent necessity of deduction in hypothesis testing, the H-D method is prone to error and ambiguity in field ecology. This circumstance obtains for ≥ 4 reasons. First, as Romesburg (1981) pointed out, it is conceivable that a true hypothesis could be rejected in H-D experimentation because some associated, unknown factor neutralized the effects of a perturbation. In a similar vein, the H-D method does not eliminate the possibility of erroneously assigning cause to associational or correlational factors rather than to true causes. By associational factors, I mean 2 events that seem to be related in a causal manner. If burning increases food supplies for an animal and density of the animal increases after fire, one might ascribe cause of the increase to food. However, a change in the structure of habitat might explain the increase just as well as or better than food, or both factors might be involved to degrees.

Second, the H-D method may falter in the presence of multiple causes for some phenomenon. Suppose we want to know what causes large antlers in cervids. We might hypothesize (H_i) and deduce (D_i) along these lines:

H_1: Genotype governs antler size. D_1: Average antler size may be altered with selective breeding.

H_2: Nutrition governs antler size. D_2: Average antler size may be altered with variable nutrition.

H_3: Age governs antler size. D_3: Up to the age of senility, antler size will be an increasing function of age.

We know these 3 hypotheses and deductions therefrom are simultaneously true. In the presence of a single hypothesis on cause, the H-D method would lead to support for the hypothesis, yet that hypothesis would be an incomplete explanation. Therefore, the H-D method potentially leads to the propagation of incomplete knowledge (fractional truths). Indeed, the H-D method might be deceptive in multicause venues, which undoubtedly are omnipresent in ecosystems. Perhaps the best that can be done is to list the causes and assess their relative importance.

The above example shows that the value of multiple hypotheses goes beyond that of protecting scientists from their ego, as Chamberlin (1890) argued. Multiple hypotheses also help protect against fractional truths possibly derived by H-D experimentation.

A third problem with H-D experimentation is that competing research hypotheses might lead to identical deductions (Guthery 2004). Hiller and Guthery (2005), for example, tested the competing hypotheses that heat avoidance versus predator avoidance governed midday covert selection by northern bobwhites. The deduced behaviors (use of robust cover for shade or protection) were identical under either hypothesis, and field research gave ambiguous results relative to the hypotheses. In the presence of a single hypothesis (heat or predators) and the absence of critical thought, however, H-D might have supported a hopelessly confounded cause as a full cause.

A fourth problem involves the drawing of conclusions from H-D experimentation; namely, that in nontrivial circumstances, there remains no faultless method for determining whether field results support or refute deductions. Romesburg's (1981) example involved the positing of a research hypothesis; the deducing of a numerical event under the hypothesis, which he called a test consequence; and the application of a significance test to assess the merit of the deduction. Under his approach, the deduction is a 1-tailed alternative to the null hypothesis. This creates the curious if not paradoxical situation that a sample-to-population induction from a statistical test is at once a deduction from a research hypothesis. Here again, we have induction and deduction being the same species.

Significance testing also brings to bear human arbitrariness in the conduct of science. For example, a difference might be construed significant at $P < 0.05$ but not at $P < 0.06$. In the limit of sample size, all differences will be significant (Johnson 1999). So, under Romesburg's approach, all test consequences might prevail and all deductions might be "true" if approached from the angle of null hypothesis significance testing with large samples. These arguments serve to further illustrate that there is no faultless method of determining support or lack thereof for deductions.

The logic that prevails in the halls of math buildings does not necessarily work in the hurly-burly of the back forty, so the natural resource scientist must apply H-D experimentation with a somewhat cynical outlook. Failure to observe a prediction does not necessarily refute a hypothesis. "There are occasions when it is the experiment you want to reject or explain away, rather than the hypothesis" (Edmonds and Eidinow 2001:244).

Retroduction
Definition
In retroduction, one views data or observations as deductions (predictions) and tries to figure out the rules or principles that would lead to those deductions had they been known beforehand. Sherlock Holmes used retroduction to solve crimes. For example, we might observe variation in animal density on different areas and retroductively hypothesize that the variation is explainable on the basis of variation in edge quantities on the different areas. Retroduction is essentially a synonym for hypothesis formulation.

Examples
Examples of retroduction often appear in the "Discussion" section of articles, where authors attempt to explain how or why their reported results occurred. Here is an example: "The smaller annual range estimates for [transplanted wild turkeys (*Meleagris gallopavo*)] than for established populations were probably due to the more restrictive way we calculated range size, and perhaps resulted from reduced social interactions and low population levels" (Little and Varland 1981:425). After the fact of study, in other words, these authors posited the existential hypothesis that "reduced social interactions lead to smaller annual ranges."

Lochmiller et al. (1994) observed temporal changes in the average immunocompetence (ability to resist disease) of wild cotton rats (*Sigmodon hispidus*). In discussion, they developed the retroductive hypotheses that temporal shifts in genetic polymorphisms caused temporal changes in immunocompetence.

Delehanty et al. (2004:591) provide another example of retroduction. They observed descriptively that mountain quail (*Oreortyx pictus*) tended to show high fidelity to specific guzzlers (artificial watering devices). This high fidelity was the event in need of explanation after the fact. They advanced 2 causal hypotheses: (1) "Mountain quail may be sedentary year-round, and a particular guzzler serves as a primary water source within the home range." (2) "Mountain quail limit their movements during the late-summer period of thermal stress due to unfamiliarity with other water sources."

The common property of all retroductions is that an event or observation has been recorded. Thereafter, hypotheses are formulated on the existence of some relationship (whether), the process that explains the event (how), or the cause of the event (why). These retroductive hypotheses may become research hypotheses in a follow-up study.

Philosophical Considerations

Philosophers regard retroductive reasoning as the form of reasoning most prone to error. Accordingly, no retroductive argument is to be trusted until challenged by further experimentation. Perhaps the main problem with retroduction is that, as mentioned above, different causes can lead to the same effect and an effect might have multiple causes. Therefore, it is a good idea to put forth competing retroductive hypotheses that are consistent with accepted knowledge. (Often it is quite difficult to form a list of competing hypotheses on cause.) Whereas retroduction may be the weakest form of reasoning, it is the form that leads to originality in science. Induction is pedestrian, and deduction involves the testing of hypotheses already formulated.

Use of Reasoning in Research

Before applying induction, deduction, or retroduction, consider the nature of your research project. Is it a simple descriptive natural history study? Are you simply measuring the magnitude of some known effect such that reasoning is moot? Are you measuring a large set of independent variables in wild-eyed hope of finding correlations? If the answer is "yes" on any of these questions, then cast the study as what it is—simple description, magnitude-of-effect estimation, or "fishing expedition." Do not make gratuitous predictions as if they were deductions in these types of studies: "we predicted a significant difference," "we predicted an increase in . . . ," "we predicted this would be larger than that." These are mindless predictions that fail statistical confirmation only with insufficient sampling.

Usually it is legitimate and desirable to test the inductive find-ings of other researchers. If study A reveals an inductive pattern, then we might challenge the inductive pattern in study B. This is a test of an inductive premise with independent data. For example, if one study reveals that a habitat variable is predictive of the location of nest sites, then that variable may be tested in a second study. Like-wise, if one study generates a predictive or relational model, then that model, inductively derived, predicts events that will occur in a second study.

The testing of "how" or "why" hypotheses is based on the H-D thought process structured as follows:

1. An event or pattern raises questions as to cause or explanation.

2. The scientist formulates hypotheses to explain how or why the event or pattern occurs.

3. The scientist deduces events or patterns that will occur or circumstances that must exist if the hypotheses are true.

4. The scientist conducts an experiment to determine whether the deductions hold.

Perspectives

This chapter should make you aware of a major disconnect between canons of the philosophy of science and the practice of natural re-source science. Philosophers and logicians hold that an induction is forever on trial, yet the practice of field science necessitates wholesale use of induction to grow knowledge. Where does this leave us? One thing to bear in mind is that natural resource scientists can invoke human judgment regarding the quality of an induction. That judg-ment is a composite of all knowledge and experience that may be brought to bear on a question. There is no like circumstance in formal logic; therefore, the philosophers' view of induction is sterile relative to that of practicing scientists. "That belief gradually tends to fix itself under the influence of inquiry," observed Peirce (2000:1354), "is . . . one of the facts with which logic sets out."

On the other hand, the philosophers view deduction as the same as truth (that is essentially how they define a deduction). Ac-cordingly, they recommend the H-D method as a means of assessing the verity of hypotheses. Yet in field application the H-D method has multiple flaws that may render the results of an experiment inconclusive or even misleading. Here again, the scientist must bring knowledge and experience to bear on a question and apply judgment. The main redeeming feature of the H-D method is that it is the only way to test research hypotheses.

Retroduction is the same as hypothesis formulation. One danger of retroduction is that hypotheses so formulated will not be tested and will be taken as true. This was one of Romesburg's (1981) concerns.

In the final analysis, induction is not necessarily bad and deduction is not necessarily good as methods of knowledge accrual and confirmation in natural resource science. Ironically, deduction cannot happen without induction or retroduction. The axioms of formal logic perform poorly, if at all, in the field. Accordingly, practicing natural resource scientists have no alternative but to *judge* whether their findings and ideas are meritorious. An understanding of the nature of facts, the subject of the next chapter, is a useful adjunct to rendering reliable judgments.

CHAPTER 4

The Nature of Facts

> *Statements of fact are not all true or all false.*
> —Bart Kosko (1993:8)

> *[A] fact or datum, by itself, is essentially meaningless; it is only the*
> interpretation *assigned to it that has significance.*
> —Robert Rosen (1991:17; emphasis in original)

> *It is quite conceivable that everyone might agree and yet be wrong about the way*
> *the world is.*
> —Sam Harris (2005:180).

Science is, among other things, a search for facts about the status and properties of nature. Collected facts serve as the foundation for more elegant knowledge on the patterns and processes of nature. So, to conduct natural resource science in a manner that leads to reliable knowledge, we should have a clear idea of the nature and properties of facts.

A dictionary might define a fact as "the state of things as they are; reality; actuality; truth." As I will argue, this is a rather optimistic definition because facts so defined may hold only for certain existential statements and the theorems of mathematics and logic (Kosko 1992). Many facts used by natural resource scientists arise through processes that may be messy and misleading in field ecology: induction, deduction, and retroduction (chapter 3). Indeed, facts are to some degree aggrandizements of the ideas gained from these processes. The word *fact,* when applied to hypotheses or inductions, makes these concepts seem more substantive than they may be. All facts outside of logical deductions are marred by the circumstance that they exist only by virtue of human agreement, and humans are the worst (indeed, the only!) enemy of objectivity.

This chapter discusses the general nature of facts. I contrast beliefs and facts and point out these concepts may commingle in the same version of "truth." I categorize facts as falling into 2 classes, one acceptable and one riddled with conditions. I discuss the conditions that render accepted facts provisional.

Definition and Nature

Facts are phenomena of consensus, meaning at least some people agree that they are facts and not fantasies. Common usage of the word *fact* is simply an abbreviation for the phrase "a phenomenon of consensus." Ziman (1978:6) maintained that scientific facts are consensual (scientists agree) and consensible (scientists have a common understanding).

Phenomena of consensus fall into at least 2 general classes: cultural facts or beliefs (e.g., aliens abduct and probe humans) and accultural facts (e.g., $E = mc^2$). Beliefs originate from the human imagination and spread among minds via meme (thought) replication (Dawkins 1976; Blackmore 1999). Religion and politics, among other social institutions, deal with beliefs, which tend to be culturally endemic. That is, beliefs do not easily cross cultural boundaries. Facts also originate from the human imagination, but they are constrained by observations of and measurements from nature; facts also spread by meme replication. Science deals with accultural facts, which are culturally pandemic (cross cultural boundaries).

People "believe in" things in the absence of logic and experience to support them. Scientists "accept" facts in the presence of logic and experience to support them. I hope that no scientists "believe in" any aspect of science, but rather tentatively "accept" notions under a veil of doubt and skepticism. Of course, adherents of various nonscientific enterprises, such as religion, politics, and astrology, believe that they deal in facts. They do but only to the extent that their facts lack support in logic and experience, and they lack a veil of doubt and skepticism.

Belief and fact may, unfortunately, hybridize in the practice of science. Leopold's (1933:132) law of dispersion (principle of edge), for example, belongs to the set of beliefs as well as to the set of facts. That is, the "law" has elements of accultural truth (Guthery and Bingham 1992), but it also has become a belief through repetition (Giles 1978:139). Other principles that have accultural and cultural aspects include the concepts of biodiversity (it's good), interspersion (it's good), and exotic species (they're bad) as they relate to ecological individuals, populations, and communities.

Scientific facts may be classified into at least 2 fairly crisp sets. The first class includes something known to exist or demonstrated to have existed. Salmon migrate. The bird fed its young at 0800 on June 11. Quail eat seeds. We shall call these Class I facts. Such facts do not engender argument from rational human beings because the facts are matters of history and not preconception.

The second class of facts might be described as matters of objective reality. A better (if somewhat cumbersome) way to view such facts is "matters deemed by consensus to be matters of objective reality." Facts in this class may be wrong, or if not wrong, they always carry conditions under which they are true. It is difficult not to conclude that the facts in this class are, without exception, deficient in one way or another. We shall call them Class II facts, which seems appropriate in a literal and figurative sense.

Deficiencies of Class II Facts

The student should keep in mind that the deficiencies listed below do not necessarily all apply to any particular fact, but one or more of the properties apply to most Class II facts. Henceforth I will simply call Class II facts "facts."

Contingency

Many of the facts we deal with in natural resource science probably are contingent. This means any statement of fact may carry with it the baggage of implicit (not recognized) or explicit (recognized) assumption. Consider, for example, these seemingly crisp and culturally transcendent facts:

* The acceleration due to gravity of an object is 9.8 m/sec/sec. Implicit assumptions (among others): the gravitational attraction is that of Earth or an object of identical mass under free fall in a vacuum.

* The shortest distance between 2 points is a straight line. Implicit assumption: the universe of discourse is Euclidean (flat) as opposed to non-Euclidean (curved) space.

* The average body mass of a species is 3.2 kg. Implicit condition: latitude is known because mass varies with latitude.

The above statements are true only if assumptions or conditions are specified. They are false if assumptions or conditions fail.

Relativity

The contingency of facts differs but subtly from their relativity. Contingency and relativity possibly should be pooled as a common property. I argue, however, there is heuristic value in highlighting assumption as a foundation for fact (contingency) and state of a system as a foundation for fact (relativity).

Consider the lethal ambient temperature for a small bird. We could state as fact that these temperatures are lethal: 39.5 °C, 40.0 °C,

40.5 °C, and so on. Indeed, researchers might report these temperatures as the ambient temperature that is lethal to the bird, leading to
conflicting facts in the literature. All of the reports would be true and
false. The key need from the standpoint of science is an understanding
of the functional relation (pattern) between death from hyperthermia,
time of exposure to high temperatures, thermal properties (e.g., mass,
coloration) of the subject, humidity, and wind speed, that is,

lethal temperature = f(temperature, time, thermal properties,
humidity, wind speed).

A specific answer to the question, What is the lethal temperature for the bird? is perforce relative to the conditions (temperature,
time, thermal properties, humidity, wind speed) leading to the estimate. Actually, the equation describing upper lethal temperature as
a function of 5 variables is the entity of scientific interest. Ecology
has many questions best answered with an equation; answering them
with anything more specific leads to contradiction and confusion.
Nonetheless, the temperature question illustrates how facts may hold
only relative to the state of a system, as further illustrated below.

Facts of measurement from the field may be products of multivariate, curvilinear systems composed of interacting variables. There
may well be universal truths associated with the system; indeed, the
system may be a universal truth. However, when biologists extract
particulars from the system, a fact here might contradict a fact there
despite sampling in the same system. In short, facts may be relative to
the state of the system when the facts are derived or contrived.

Guthery, King, et al. (2001) provided an example of how relativity might accrue in field studies. Their goal was to develop a model
that discriminated between habitat patches used by masked bobwhites (*C. v. ridgwayi;* an endangered race of the northern bobwhite)
and randomly available patches. Data were collected on operative
temperature, exposure of bare ground, canopy coverage of woody
vegetation, exposure to ground predators, and exposure to aerial
predators at used and random patches. These were the 5 independent
variables used to develop a prediction model. The data were analyzed
with neural modeling, a powerful multivariate technique that deals
easily with nonlinear relations. The neural model that resulted was a
complex equation that predicted a numerical score ranging between
0 and 1. If the score was below 0.5, a patch was classified as random;
scores above 0.5 indicated used patches.

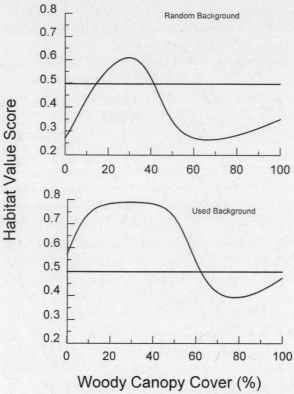

Fig. 4-1 Habitat value scores for masked bobwhites in Sonora, Mexico, when independent variables other than woody canopy cover were held constant at the means for random points (random background) versus the means for used points (used background). The same equation governed these relationships.

The neural model developed for masked bobwhites in Sonora, Mexico, correctly discriminated patch types (used versus random) at a rate of about 80% on training and validation data based on a sample of 601 points. This means that a governing equation, as approximated by the neural model, held generally for masked bobwhites in Sonora. (The model may be used to illustrate the relativity of facts independent of whether it was a good approximation of reality.)

The discrimination score for masked bobwhite patches based upon canopy coverage of woody vegetation (Fig. 4-1) illustrates how perception of fact depends on context. If we hold operative temperature, exposure of bare ground, and exposure to predators constant at mean values from randomly selected points, we obtain the discrimination image in the top graph. On the other hand, if we hold these variables constant at mean values for used (bobwhite-occurrence points), we get the image in the bottom graph.

Suppose 2 different studies examine optimal coverage values of woody vegetation for masked bobwhites. If one takes place in habitat approximating the random mean background for other variables, and if one takes place in habitat approximating the used mean background, conflicting results will ensue. The first study will indicate optimal coverage is in the range 15%–40%; optimal range in the second study will be 0%–60%. Note that the conflicting results accrue from the same governing equation. The results of both studies are valid, given the context from which data were drawn. Truth is relative to the state of the system.

Ambiguity

The ambiguity of a fact may be likened to its fuzziness. Fuzzy logicians permit the truth-value of a statement to range between 0 (false) and 1 (true) (Kosko 1992). This is in contrast to Aristotelian logic, in which statements are either true or false. Facts may have a truth-value of 1 on a 0–1 scale, given their contingent nature—$1 + 1 = 2$ has a truth-value of 1 under assumptions. Most facts have a truth-value <1 (they are to some degree false). ("Most" is a troubling qualifier, because the set of contingent facts with truth-value 1 has infinitely many elements, as does the set of contingent facts with truth value <1. How do you deal with "more" or "fewer" when you are dealing with infinities? Perhaps the proper response is simply to consider all facts suspect.)

Here is an example of a fact with truth value <1: grass is green (Kosko 1992:269). The little bluestem (*Schizochyrium scoparius*) in central Oklahoma is approximately pink, and the yellow Indiangrass (*Sorghastrum nutans*) is straw colored during winter. The green of bermudagrass (*Cynodon dactylon*) differs from the green of fescue (*Festuca* sp.) during the growing season. Thus, the statement "grass is green" is to some degree true and to some degree false.

Wildlife scientists use fuzzy facts as a matter of rote. A good example is the arbitrary distinction between *r*- and *K*-selected species. A bobwhite would be called an *r*-selected species, but it is not *r*-selected to the same degree as a deer mouse (*Peromyscus* sp.) or bacterium. So relative to a deer mouse, a bobwhite is to some degree *K*-selected, but not to the degree of whales.

Speciousness

Compare the possible fact, density-dependent predation stabilizes wildlife populations, with another possible fact, density-dependent predator avoidance stabilizes populations. In the first case, cause emanates from predators; in the second case, it emanates from prey (as through fitness and learned behaviors). In either case, we would observe the same population behavior, and either "fact" would explain the behavior. We could conceivably "understand" the world based on the wrong "fact" and never have cause to question ourselves.

As another example, bobwhites may increase with prescribed burning of southeastern forests. Due to Stoddard's (1931) research, the assumption has always been that increased food supplies, especially legumes, were responsible for the increases. Burning, however, creates more usable space (acceptable permanent cover) by reducing woody biomass, and there is reason to believe usable space governs bobwhite population abundance to a greater degree than food supplies (Guthery 1997, 2002). Because in southeastern forests the quantity of foods is correlated with the quantity of usable space, management could operate under the wrong idea of cause-effect process and be successful in some applications. Management failure could ensue, however, upon extrapolation of the false premise to different environments or to specific management programs.

Specious facts are fictions that may predict quite well. The hallmarks of specious facts are these: (1) a passive variable (e.g., food supplies) is correlated with a driving variable (e.g., usable space) or (2) >2 conceivable processes or circumstances lead to identical outcomes (e.g., density-dependent predation versus density-dependent predator avoidance).

Although false facts that work may seem innocuous, they are philosophically deplorable. Science is a search for truth, not an adventure in expediency. Moreover, specious facts may not generalize to new contexts, thus leading to misinterpretation, misapplication, confusion, and contradiction.

Ambivalence

Like love-hate relationships, certain facts are defined by contradictory concepts, by polarities. I call them yin-yang facts. For example, the insulative capacity of a material defines its conductive capacity and vice versa, mortality defines survival and vice versa, additive mortality defines compensatory mortality and vice versa. All information in a yin-yang fact is contained in the concept at one or the other of the poles; that is, an equation can be developed that expresses either pole in terms of the other. You can, for example, express insulative capacity in terms of conductivity and vice versa or compensatory mortality in terms of additive mortality and vice versa (Guthery 2002).

There is nothing wrong with yin-yang facts per se. However, when scientists fail to recognize they are dealing with a yin-yang fact, endless debate and controversy may ensue even though everybody is arguing about degrees of the same thing. Whether harvest mortality in game populations is additive or compensatory is a good example of the controversy that a yin-yang fact may engender. Compensation and additivity define different poles along the same concept; between the poles, harvest mortality is at once additive and compensatory (Guthery 2002:96).

Evanescence
Because of consensuality, relativity, contingency, ambivalence, and ambiguity, it should not be surprising that facts may have short lives. Facts would seem to be especially vulnerable to extinction in the early stages of a science. Those that remain in the late stages are either the beliefs of scientific cults, or they have survived a brutal selection process and gained a consensus because their contingencies were few and their ambiguities minor.

The breeding biology of northern bobwhites provides an example of a fact that died and went to fiction (which we take to be the homologue of hell for fallen facts). With arrogance bordering on hubris, Davison (1949:37–38) averred, "A few people still believe quail may raise [2] broods of young in [1] year. . . . [Herbert L.] Stoddard called this a false idea [20] years ago for Georgia and Florida. [Paul L.] Errington echoed the proof in Iowa in 1932. We found it untrue beyond doubt for Oklahoma in 1932, '33, '34, and '35." At the start of the third millennium, double brooding is known to be a common behavior in bobwhites, including those in Oklahoma (Sermons and Speake 1987; Taylor 1991; Curtis et al. 1993; DeVos and Mueller 1993; Suchy and Munkel 1993; Burger et al. 1995; Cox et al. 2005). Ziman (1978:64) recommended a good deal of circumspection when a scientist communicates a fact. The example of bobwhite breeding behavior illustrates why.

Of course, given the nature of facts, it might be possible for one to rise from the killing fields of fiction. In field ecology, moreover, it is sometimes difficult to tell whether the data support or disprove some conjecture (the curse of nondemonic variation; Hurlbert 1984). Thus, the evidence for discarding a fact should be strong before it is discarded.

If the evidence is strong enough, then the fact should be filed under human error and used only as an example of the pitfalls in pursuit of truth. Clinging to fallen facts serves neither natural resources nor the profession they support (Guthery 2002). Certainly, fallen facts have no business in science, for a strong protocol of science is the abandonment of fact become fantasy (Feynman 1998:16).

The Compleat Skeptic

If facts are "the state of things as they are," then we rarely, if ever, deal with pure facts in natural resource science. Rather, we generally deal with conditional facts or fuzzy facts that might be defined as "the state of things as they are to some degree." There is nothing unusual about our science in this respect. "All information is imperfect" (Bronowski 1973:353; except, we presume, Bronowski's information).

Accordingly, the proper perspective for scientists is skepticism over that which passes for fact or knowledge (Sagan 1997:139). Doubting rather than accepting, rebelling rather than conforming, and refuting rather than supporting exemplify skepticism.

Critical reading of scientific papers also exemplifies skepticism. Critical reading is hard work, for it involves a detailed assay of linkages in a paper, from objectives through methods, results, discussion, and conclusions. Are the linkages logical, supported with data, free of human value? A critical reader draws conclusions based on the data presented and then checks to see whether those conclusions match the ones tendered by authors. A critical reader is sensitive to waves of sentiment (e.g., biodiversity, the damning of exotic species) that sweep through the ranks of eco-thinkers. Such a reader cynically assumes that reported conclusions will support the human sentiment if not the state of nature, because human beings are notoriously vulnerable to mass illusion (March 1994:40; Brothers 1997:75), especially when a mode of thinking is trendy. Critical readers will compare affiliation of authors with their conclusions, for the conclusions of wildlife studies often can be predicted based on that affiliation (Smith 1988). In such cases, the skeptic wonders whether technical merit of the research or vested interest of the supporting entity most influenced results.

Perspectives

A key point of this chapter is that from the scientific perspective there is an important distinction between beliefs and facts. Beliefs, as defined here, lack support in logic and experience and carry no veil of skepticism and doubt. Scientific facts have such support and a veil of skepticism and doubt. There is a troubling propensity of humans to commingle belief and fact. Scientists commit this error, which is dangerous behavior in pursuit of reliable knowledge.

Broadly speaking, there are 2 classes of fact with different levels of trustworthiness. Natural resource scientists can perhaps trust Class I (existential) facts, such as "birds migrate," but they cannot fully trust Class II facts (those that purportedly deal in objective reality), such as "the shortest distance between 2 points is a straight line." Class II facts seem invariably to be propped up by assumptions or conditions, perhaps unknown ones, and hence prevail over a limited realm of discourse. Class II facts might even be false when correlation is taken as cause or when different hypotheses, only one of which is true, lead to the same deduction.

"Facts" from the scientific perspective may be partially trustworthy, at best. When facts are viewed under the pall of human sociality, they may become even less trustworthy. "We have agendas (not necessarily political ones, I hasten to add) in pursuing the truth, and this will always raise the question of how true that 'truth' really is" (Berman 2000:177). Those agendas are part of the human, subjective side of science, the topic of the next chapter.

CHAPTER 5 **Being Humans**

It is common to explain historic events after the fact in terms of the preoccupation of the historian. Thus the economist finds his pattern in economics, the politician in politics, and the medical man in pollens or parasites.
—John Steinbeck (1994:129)

Belonging is a primary human motivation: In order to belong, individuals adopt and use the narratives that surround them.
—Leslie Brothers (1997:82)

The way we experience the world is not "the way it really is" but the way that has proved useful to natural selection for us to perceive it.
—Susan Blackmore (1999:112)

Here is a sampling of newspaper headlines from March 10, 2006: "Truck Blast Kills Seven Iraqis." "Pakistani Bus Blast Kills 26." "Afghan Terrorists Kill Policeman in Gun Battle." "Nine Die in Suicide Pact." "Alcohol May Have Fueled Alabama Church Fires." "Chinese Catholic Leader Condemns Vatican for Anti-communist Cardinal." "Michael Jackson Fined over Neverland Labor Miscue." "American Idol Axes Four." "Syracuse Boots UConn in Big East." "New Animal Resembles Furry Lobster."

The species that generated these headlines is the same one that aspires to practice natural resource science. The headlines implicitly contain statements on the human condition, and those statements cut across the proletariat, the bourgeoisie, and the aristocracy of thought. All of the killing has roots in sectarianism and myth. It is inevitable that natural resource scientists hold myths because the scientists are members of the human species. Humans of all stations readily subscribe to the cockamamie if it is traditional, trendy, or tribal.

In an odd way, the headlines also contain statements on the intense sociality of *Homo sapiens*. This sociality leads to the tribal behavior that runs contrary to logic, common sense, and empirical virtue, and it is the major mental handicap of the species in its pursuit of scientific truth. *Sapiens* also has severe physiological handicaps that constrict the breadth of incoming sensory data, which obviously constricts the breadth of information that can be drawn from nature. The species has a marvelous brain. That brain is insufficient, however, for dealing with all but the surface of reality. It is a brain with quirks that apparently served cavepersons and their hairy-tailed progenitors, but that inhibits the free flow of ideas and beclouds the perceptions of nature in scientists.

This chapter summarizes the tariffs on scientific progress levied by the human condition; these tariffs include physiological, mental, and social handicaps. I assume that if natural resource scientists know about these handicaps, they will be better able to deal with them and inject sound knowledge into mainstream thinking. I also provide some recommendations on how to deal with some human handicaps that impede progress in understanding nature.

Physiological Handicaps

Of the five senses—sight, sound, touch, smell, and taste—we gain most of the information we use in science through the eyes. We know that our vision is insufficient to observe the vast majority of physical reality, such as the ultraviolet and infrared portions of the electromagnetic spectrum, microwaves and gamma rays. "Science must often transcend sight to win insight" because "many well-documented conclusions of science lie beyond the strictly limited domain of direct observation" (Gould 1993:200). Likewise, we do not hear the infra- and ultrasonic sounds that wave through the air. Every dog owner knows there are infra and ultra portions of the nasal spectrum that are beyond human detection. Undoubtedly, nature has befitted its citizens with a gustatory spectrum that contains human ability as a slender subset of the biologically possible.

The upshot is that we are physiologically impaired for dealing with physical reality. The physicists and engineers have developed artificial methods of sensing that reality, and we apply them in everything from assaying parts per million of chemical contaminants to training dogs to reheating macaroni and cheese. Indeed, science has expanded all of our senses (Wilson 1998:47). But we still miss most of the events transpiring in nature.

Mental Handicaps

Mind and culture exacerbate the problems engendered by our physiological deficiencies. Regarding mind, which we use for creativity and conceptualizing, we have at least five maladaptations from the perspective of science: confirmation bias, linear prejudice, inattentional blindness, prototypical thinking, and bounded possibility, which I discuss in order below.

Humans and animals have a genetically based tendency to view or interpret two events closely related in time as being causally related; this is called the confirmation bias (Grandin and Johnson 2004:98). This tendency is thought to be an aid to learning because time-near events often are related in a cause-effect manner. If two such events are not causally related, superstition may ensue in both humans and animals.

The confirmation bias could well impact laboratory and field observations. That is, if we are not careful, we will tend to perceive time-near events as cause and effect. If they are not, we might end up with scientific superstition (the erroneous belief that two events are causally related).

The confirmation bias raises the more serious issue of whether scientists might have a tendency to view associated or correlated events as causally related, independent of time. We cannot be sure whether such a bias exists. The only prudent course of action, given the possibility of this more general confirmation bias, is to assume that it does exist. Therefore, scientists probably generally should be skeptical of cause-effect processes that they or other scientists advance.

Like confirmation bias, a linear mode of thinking (Kaku 1994; or passively responding to stimuli) might be a product of evolution. The verbal expression of linearity, "is proportional to," would seem a powerful implicit or explicit assumption for living and begetting: the quantity of food is proportional to the density of herbivore dung; the danger from a predator is proportional to the frequency of its spoor. The evolution of linearity in rote or reasoned responses to stimuli seems more plausible than, say, the evolution of a logistic response.

Whether the brain evolved linearity remains speculative, but there is no doubt that human exercise of brain function is largely a straight-line process. Intuition may be an is-proportional-to leap of induction. The whole of linear algebra and much of statistics (which derives from linear algebra) are drills in linear approximation and interpretation of nature. Indeed, an overwhelming emphasis on linear systems has resulted in skewed intuition and limited metaphors (i.e., linear prejudice) in the practice of science (Kellert 1993:136).

Skewed intuition and limited metaphors are the problems. "The world is not a very linear place" (Smith 1996:18). It is replete with interference (competition, predation), cooperation (e.g., mutualism), and feedback (e.g., density-dependent processes) that lead to nonlinearity in systems (Strogatz 1994:9). Scientists need to recognize they are linearly challenged by practice if not by breeding, and they must respond with an appreciation of the nature and implications of nonlinearity. Graphs and mathematics assist in dealing with nonlinearity.

A third problem is glaucoma of the mind's eye regarding that which is not known or expected beforehand, which Grandin and Johnson (2004), among other scientists, call inattentional blindness. *"Humans are built to see what they're expecting to see,* and it's hard to *expect* to see something you've never seen. New things just don't register" (Grandin and Johnson 2004:25; emphasis in original). They cite a study wherein about a quarter of commercial airline pilots in a flight simulator landed on a jetliner parked on the runway. These pilots did not expect to see a jetliner on the runway.

What we expect to see carries over into mental concepts. Goethe (1749–1832) said we see only what we know. For example, suppose we encounter a new word and look it up in a dictionary. Then, in reading or discourse, we are more likely to see or hear the word after we know it than before we knew it. The same type of thing holds for a plant or animal you have learned to identify: before you know it, you do not see it; after you know it, you may realize it is quite common. Humans have the ability to know-see and the tendency to no-see (the know-see–no-see syndrome).

The usable-space hypothesis of bobwhite management (Guthery 1997) provides a know-see–no-see example from my experience. When I developed the hypothesis in the mid-1990s, I thought it quite original and felt a rush of euphoria. However, when I understood the concept, I started seeing it in literature published in the 1930s. I didn't see (perceive) it until I saw (understood) it.

A fourth problem of mind is the universal human tendency to talk and think in prototypes (Anderson 1995:34; Pinker 1997:126), or what might be called exemplars drawn from fuzzy sets (items with the strongest degree of membership in a fuzzy set). For example, in human perception, orange is a stronger member of the fuzzy set "fruit" than olive, pea a stronger member of "vegetable" than rice, and robin a stronger member of "bird" than penguin (Rosch 1975; Rosch probably was not aware of fuzzy membership functions, but her results lend themselves to fuzzy set theory). Thus, a word like *bird* has general meaning as a mental image, but that image does not encompass all birds equally nor do all humans hold the same mental image upon cogitating *bird*.

Scientists, being humans, think and communicate using exemplars with strong membership in fuzzy sets: light, moderate, and heavy grazing; compensatory and additive mortality; r- and K-selected species; lower and higher successional species; cool and hot fires, for example. Communication with exemplars creates two problems from the perspective of science: it guarantees miscommunication because one person's exemplar might be another's outlier, and it deflects awareness from the underlying continua that generate fuzzy exemplars. The continua become vague recollections, if not forgotten altogether. Unfortunately, the continua—not the fuzzy exemplars—contain the key information about understanding nature.

Kaplan (2000:160) summed up bounded possibility, a fifth handicap: "The world may not only be more singular [remarkable] than we think, it may be more singular than we *can* think" (emphasis in original). Our intellectual capacity is bounded. "The more of reality we comprehend, the more aware we become of horizons that keep receding before us and are as unattainable as the peripheries of the expanding universe" (Eigen and Winkler 1981:187).

Attempts to think in the fourth or higher dimensions readily illustrate the problem. We can deal analytically with higher dimensions in linear systems, as linear algebra demonstrates, but we cannot understand what is going on. For example, Kleinbaum (1994:170) observed that 3-way interactions in logistic regression modeling might not be interpretable, that attempts to understand higher-order interactions are hopeless. Biologists might take comfort in knowing that even theoretical physicists are dimensionally challenged. Hawking (1988:24) admits to bewilderment in 3-dimensional space.

Social Handicaps

Stifling effects of the foibles mentioned above pale in comparison with those produced by our urge to be upstanding members of the tribe. Our allegiance to conspecifics, our sociality, our drive to belong is more than a weakness in the culture of science; it is a genuine character flaw. The flaw guarantees that if we are not extremely skeptical of ourselves, we are more likely to see support for group mores than objective truth in our research results.

The flaw is deeply ingrained in our biology. "Monkeys, apes, and humans must all gear their behavior to that of other members of the group in which they live," observed Brothers (1997:27–28). Socially responsive neurons in the brain mandate this response, at least to some degree. We are, to use the vernacular, hardwired to be social. As a result of biocircuits switched on by, say, facial features (Brothers 1997:36), "people seem to seek not certainty of knowledge but social validity" (March 1994:40). Pause and reflect on March's statement. Ponder to what degree those of us in natural resource science seek social validity rather than certainty of knowledge.

A recent study documented the power of the group on the perception of individuals (Berns et al. 2005). A group of 5 people including 1 experimental subject and 4 actors were shown computer images of 2 identical geometric shapes, one rotated from the other. The subjects were to determine whether the images represented the same shape, and the actors always gave the wrong answer. When the subjects were tested in the absence of the actors, their error rate was about 15%. The error rates jumped to 41% in the presence of the actors (who were giving the wrong answer).

Thus, group influence caused the error rate of experimental subjects to increase. The question is whether the subjects were "just going along with the crowd" or whether their perceptions changed. Brain-imaging results suggested that the group influenced the *perceptions* of the subjects (Berns et al. 2005). It would be induction most indecent to suppose that the results of this single study hold over the human experience. However, it is chilling to contemplate that people might cause themselves to see what the group sees, even when the group is wrong.

Scientific behavior that can be construed as the pursuit of social validity is easy to demonstrate in natural resource science (or any human vocation except schizophrenia, for that matter). An apparent example from the annals of bobwhite research involves Errington and Hamerstrom's (1935) postulate of a threshold of security that governs the abundance of bobwhite populations in spring. Existence of the threshold implies a doomed surplus of individuals, and thus harvest mortality would be fully compensatory over a range of harvest intensities; that is, harvest doesn't matter. I suspect the threshold concept was quite popular (and socially valid) when it appeared because it sanctioned the recreational harvest of bobwhites; it justified not only the programs of state game departments but also the behavior of hunter-managers who must have felt ambivalent about loving the animals they killed and killing the animals they loved. Under a threshold, the killing could be construed as compatible with the love if one placed value upon the population instead of the individual.

The popularity of the threshold concept apparently blinded researchers to the certainty of knowledge contained in the data they collected on the effects of harvest on bobwhite populations. Accordingly, Glading and Saarni (1944) reported no effect of harvest on California quail (*Callipepla californicus*) populations, despite the fact that fall-spring mortality averaged 47.0% on a hunted area and 28.9% on an experimental control (4 years of data). Likewise, Baumgartner (1944) observed average fall-spring mortality of 55.5% and 26.5% for bobwhites on harvest and control areas (4 years of data); he also reported that harvest had no population effect. A scientist not under the possible sway of a popular idea would look at the results of these studies and conclude that harvest roughly doubled fall-spring mortality. Parmalee (1953) provided a widely cited conclusion that bobwhite harvest did not seriously reduce bobwhite abundance. He had no sound experimental data upon which to base the conclusion. Certainty of knowledge, or social validity?

An extraordinary example of what could be construed as tribe allegiance trumping reason in natural resource science became apparent around the turn of the second millennium. Cherry (1998) and Johnson (1999) pointed out that null hypothesis significance testing was at best an ill-conceived approach to science. This was not news. Misgivings about the null hypothesis had been around for several years (Morrison and Henkel 1970). However, it seems the null hypothesis had so caught the fancy of the scientific community that literally thousands of significance tests were appearing in any given volume of technical journals, such as *Ecology* and *The Journal of Wildlife Management* (Anderson et al. 2000). Often there was no information provided other than the results of significance tests—in other words there were no numerical data such as means. Such results were beyond interpretation relative to ecological process.

Moreover, many of the tests were mindless, such as whether the density of trees in logged areas differed significantly from the density in natural areas (Johnson 1999). Although one might be able to hypothesize alternative causes for the dull-null fiasco, social imperatives of the group remain a strong candidate.

Countermeasures

"The human brain was not evolved with science in mind" (Barrow 1998:vii). Our physiological shortcomings, confirmation bias, linear prejudice, inattentional blindness, prototypical thinking, and

bounded possibilities reflect some few million years of gene propagation during which attention to our next meal or to our next tryst
displaced attention to our next hypothesis. Our social responsive-
ness reflects some few million years of inculcation on the rewards of
orthodoxy and the dangers of heterodoxy. In sum, our evolutionary
history curses us as scientists, but that does not mean we lack means
of reversing evolution's effects, at least regarding some aspects of scientific behavior.

Medical science has developed an experimental methodology
to thwart human influence: the double-blind study, which is used to
test the effects of drugs. The patients receiving drugs, including place-
bos, do not know which drug they are receiving. Likewise, the doctors
administering and evaluating drugs do not know which drug they
are dealing with. The double-blind protocol reduces the chance for
influence by human preconceptions of drug efficacy as well as human
desire to find drug efficacy. That desire might arise from the hope of
further funding from the company that manufactures a drug. I know
of no like procedures in natural resource science, but such procedures
might be developed in the future.

The culture of science has developed values to deal with the
foibles of its members. A primary value is scrupulous honesty in the
interpretation and presentation of research results. This eliminates
neither error nor human bias, but it sets a gold standard for conduct
that might thwart some of our maladaptations. Another value is a
posture of challenge to, rather than support of, existing knowledge;
we know that knowledge contains flaws, and we seek to discover
those flaws. The thought experiment (chapter 7) is a handy method
of challenge. A related value is skepticism; if readers accept the above
arguments on the nature of human nature, they should have no
trouble adopting a skeptical attitude toward extant knowledge. That
knowledge is without doubt impure because it arose from a species genetically programmed to follow the tribe and because we have ample
evidence of tribe allegiance in the exercise of natural resource science.
Finally, scientists may attempt to break out of the social humdrum of
science by creative means, the subject of the next chapter.

Perspectives

Humans have three primary handicaps as scientists: (1) their sensory
perception is limited relative to the stimuli that surround them;
(2) their mental abilities are limited; and (3) their sociality creates a

strong tendency to perceive nature according to group mores (group-think), even to the point of accepting premises that are demonstrably wrong. The sociality handicap is by far the greatest detriment to the growing of trustworthy knowledge. Scrupulous honesty, a posture of challenge to existing ideas, and skepticism over knowledge are values scientists have adopted to counteract these handicaps.

CHAPTER 6 Creativity

Every human achievement is the result of an initial act of creativity.
—Ron Hale-Evans (2006:71)

[T]he human brain is genetically disposed toward organization, yet if not tightly controlled, will link one imagerial fragment to another on the flimsiest of pretense and in the most freewheeling manner, as if it takes a kind of organic pleasure in creative association, without regard for logic or chronological sequence.
—Tom Robbins (2000:7)

What facilitates thought impoverishes imagination.
—Robert Kaplan (2000:34)

Creativity is a hallmark of the human condition. We know human creativity started at least 40,000 years ago (probably much earlier) with cave paintings by Cro-Magnons. By the late twentieth century, it gave us The Beatles and Bob Dylan. You see my bias here. The bluebloods among us might think of creativity in terms of Mozarts and Renoirs, Shakespeares and Einsteins. Indeed, we often think the trail to creativity is marked by the spoor of genius, but creativity is prevalent among us tomfools, too. We see it in everything from country-and-western songs to Superbowl commercials. Creativity improves the quality of our lives and fosters progress, and it is no less important in science than in the general human experience.

If science did not have creative input, scientists would end up studying the same things into the indefinite future. Under this scenario, knowledge accumulation would slow to a dribble; new knowledge would consist of finer and finer detail on matters mostly known and understood. Science would be quite boring. It is possible that, in the limit, science would effectively end without creativity. That would be too bad for scientists and too bad for the consumers of scientific information.

Moreover, the knowledge amassed in the absence of creativity would to some extent be incomplete and misleading. These problems would occur because, for example, a creative act in science is to discover new and better interpretations of nature, such that old and incomplete beliefs are eliminated. Scientists make mistakes, and those mistakes might persist unless challenged by creative alternatives.

The purpose of this chapter is to discuss creativity in natural resource science. I start with examples of creative acts to show certain goals of creativity. I then turn to inhibitors (especially knowledge) and releasers of creativity and discuss how to set up creative thoughts.

Examples of Creative Acts

To be creative, you must first have examples of creative acts so that you will know your goal. The following list provides several examples from natural resource science; the list undoubtedly is incomplete, but the examples are important.

1. Recognize a pattern in nature that no one has ever recognized. Mendeleev's periodic table of the elements (chapter 1) provides an example.

2. Ask a question about nature that nobody has ever thought to ask. Albert Einstein is said to have asked, "What would the clock in the town square look like if I was traveling away from it at the speed of light?" He realized that time would stand still, and he formalized the thinking in his theories of relativity. It is surprisingly difficult to bring something commonplace to thought consciousness. If that step can be taken, the next question may be how or why. Those questions may lead to original ideas.

3. Discover a useful method of classifying objects or phenomena. Sometimes it is mentally trying to organize ideas in a manner that is accurate and general. Such organization requires the same type of thinking you use when developing a lucid outline for a paper. The Linnaean system of nomenclature is not exactly the type of classification I am implying. The original idea of classifying organisms was, well, quite original, but the classification per se was rather mechanical.

A good example of inspired classification comes from linguistics. Somebody recognized a pattern in the several tens of thousands of words that make up the English language, namely, that all the words could be classified into 8 types. These are the parts of speech: nouns, pronouns, verbs, adjectives, adverbs, conjunctions, prepositions, and interjections. Whoever realized that words could be so classed made an original, brilliant discovery.

4. Discover new interpretations of old beliefs and principles; disprove old beliefs (dogma) and principles. This is sometimes a matter of simply negating some concept and thinking through the consequences of such negation. For example, density-dependent

predator avoidance is a sort of negative of density-dependent predation. These two concepts might result in the same observed population processes, but each concept changes the way we interpret
population dynamics.

5. Develop multiple research hypotheses to explain how or
why some event came to pass. Our tendency is to stop thinking
when the first explanatory idea leaps into consciousness. Scientists
must, therefore, consciously force themselves to ponder further in
hopes of finding alternative ideas.

6. Deduce outcomes under research hypotheses. At times,
this activity is menial, but depending on the hypothesis, it can be
intensely cerebral. Under the hypothesis "they need more food," a
deduction is "there will be more of them if I provide food." Deductions such as this are a primitive species of creativity. On the other
hand, deductions generated on the basis of multiple constructs can
be quite demanding from a mental standpoint. Multiple constructs
involve phenomena such as the shapes of relations and assumptions
on states of nature. The thinking process is approximately, "If this
and this and this and this . . . , then this."

7. Generate a Poincaré hypothesis. Recall that a Poincaré
hypothesis is a purely mental, abstract concept that is useful in
explaining or understanding nature. Examples are the threshold of
security, the niche as an *n*-dimensional hypervolume, and slack in
the configuration of habitat patches (chapter 2).

8. Develop a hypothesis that unifies (explains) contradictory
observations. Suppose 2 authors report different results for some
observation from the field. The contradiction could imply that both
are wrong, one or the other is correct, or both are correct. If the latter is the case, then an original, unifying hypothesis or hypotheses
await discovery. The discovery of a contradiction in the published
literature might be your ticket to creativity.

9. Search for meaning in anomalies. Anomalies or outliers in
data sets might be a vehicle for creativity. The natural tendency is to
ignore the anomalies in favor of the pattern shown by the bulk of
the data and accepted knowledge. Yet there might be useful information in aberrant observations (or they might simply be aberrant).
The point is to think about them when you run across them and try
to determine if further thought and research are in order.

Inhibitors of Creativity

Recognizing that the human species has cognitive limits that render certain concepts imponderable (chapter 5), we can say that knowledge is probably the main inhibitor of creativity. Palahniuk (2001:149) beautifully captures the problem:

> For one flash, the Mommy had seen the mountain without thinking of logging and ski resorts and avalanches, managed wildlife, plate tectonic geology, microclimates, rain shadow, or yin-yang locations. She'd seen the mountain without the framework of language. Without the cage of associations. She'd seen it without looking through the lens of everything she knew was true about mountains.
>
> What she'd seen in that flash wasn't even a "mountain." It wasn't a natural resource. It had no name.
>
> "That's the big goal," she said. "To find a cure for knowledge."

Knowledge suppresses creativity (Loehle 1990) because we universally submit to the governance of our thinking by the ideas and images already in our minds (Dewey 1910:19). The whole of university education from baccalaureate through doctoral degree could be viewed as an exercise in the suppression of creativity because it fills the mind with fixed thoughts (i.e., knowledge). Knowledge permits egress from the mind only of established ideas and blocks the appearance of new ideas.

Human ego, a second inhibitor, results in a natural tendency for individuals to see themselves, their possessions, and their ideas as above average. With respect to science, this tendency results in what Chamberlin (1890) described as self-illusion of candor on the part of scientists who generate hypotheses. Chamberlin likened the process metaphorically to parent (scientist) and child (hypothesis). Once a hypothesis has been generated (or a viewpoint taken; Vyse 1997:121), the scientist has a natural tendency to block out facts that do not support it and collect facts that do. Ego suppresses creativity by generating self-centered passion for one's own ideas and viewpoints; such passion, in turn, inhibits alternative ideas and viewpoints necessary for creative thinking.

We addressed the problem of sociality in science in chapter 5. It stifles creativity because we are more likely to see support for group mores than objective truth in or novel interpretations of our

research results, and because we do not even attempt to see phenomena not supportive of group mores. The flaw creates tabooed regions
of thought-space (where the tribe does not go); it is deeply ingrained
in our biology.

Releasers of Creativity

The first step in releasing creativity is simply recognizing the possible
causes of unimaginativeness. We can solve problems only when we
know their causes.

Several mental algorithms are available for creatively examining
old beliefs and principles and for generating new ideas and hypotheses (Hale-Evans 2006:71–126). One is the PO (provocative operation)
method, which has 3 operators. PO-1 involves protecting bad ideas
from premature judgment (keep them in mind) because these ideas
might serve as stepping stones toward better ideas; PO-1(set of ideas)
= (presumably bad ideas). PO-2 involves randomly juxtaposing ideas
to help shake you loose from preconceived notions; PO-2(randomly
juxtaposed notions) = (set of ideas derived from the notions). PO-3
involves use of this operator as a challenge to the content of ideas;
PO-3(statement) = (alternative ideas).

For example, in April 2006 I observed a ruby-throated hum-
mingbird (*Archilochus colubris*) hover in the rain of a lawn sprinkler.
Why, I wondered. I let hypotheses flow freely: it was having fun,
it was curious, it was ill, it was otherwise aberrant, it was thirsty, it
was cooling off, it was maintaining plumage (in the sense of birds
bathing), none of the above, some of the above. I preserved in mind
the presumably bad hypotheses (fun, curiosity, sickness, aberrancy)
under the PO-1 operator. PO-2(sickness, water) led to the notion
that the bird might have been febrile and was indeed cooling off.
Plumage maintenance seemed a likely hypothesis, so I calculated
PO-3(maintain) = (testing, repairing, wetting). This led me to the
hypothesis that the bird might have been testing the repellency of its
plumage in artificial rain as a hedge against a climatic rain. Whether
any of these hypotheses are meritorious is beside the point. The exercise merely illustrates the use of a mental algorithm to generate new
ideas. (After hovering, the bird lit on the ground and went through
the behavior of a bird in a birdbath.)

Another useful step in rousing creative impulses is brutal skepticism
over that which passes for fact or knowledge. Skepticism is a method

of counteracting the inhibitory properties of knowledge and social-
ization (tribe allegiance).

You can take any accepted fact and say, "I assert this is false or
incomplete." Or you can say, "This is not a fact; it is a trend, a tradition, a dogmatic outlook on the properties of nature." Or you can ask,
"Where is the evidence for this assertion?" "Slay a sacred cow" (von
Oech 1990:64), in other words. Such behavior creates self-imposed
thought-crises, and such crises may be the mother of originality.

As a case in point, the Renaissance (a time of increased curiosity
and objectivity about the world, the fourteenth to sixteenth centu-
ries) might have come about because the bubonic plague of the preceding Middle Ages shattered comfortable theological explanations
of natural law (McNeill 1998). People were compelled to rethink the
nature of nature as the plague struck down citizens on their left and
right. The Black Death invoked an overthrow of concepts and opened
mind-space for innovative thinking. Challenging the prevailing understanding of nature by arbitrarily disbelieving it is metaphorically
similar to a self-imposed plague.

Challenges to prevailing knowledge will reveal ambiguity,
which means that it is possible to hypothesize more than one process
that explains a given set of research results (Chamberlin 1890; Romesburg 1981; Guthery 2004). You can virtually assume that there exist
alternative processes that are explanatory; your goal is to dream them
up. Ambiguity is a cradle of creativity because it forces the scientist to
postulate alternative processes and to deduce events that might occur
under the alternatives. Also, the positing of multiple hypotheses is
one method of suppressing human ego (Chamberlin 1890). Multiple
hypotheses force scientists to respect all their "children" and not lav-
ish unwarranted attention on any one.

Innovative thinking, of course, requires substrate: "Other things
being equal," observed Beveridge (1957:75), "the greater our store of
knowledge, the more likely it is that significant combinations will be
thrown up. Furthermore, original combinations are more likely to
come into being if there is available a breadth of knowledge extending
into related or even *distant branches of knowledge*" (emphasis added).

"The human mind is a rich source of variation" (Blackmore
1999:15). "In our thinking, we mix up ideas and turn them over to
produce new combinations. In our dreams we mix them up even
more, with bizarre—and occasionally creative—consequences.
Human creativity is a process of variation and recombination."

Paradoxically, then, the substrate for creative thinking is knowledge. The paradox arises because knowledge at once inhibits and liberates creativity.

Here is one idea of how liberation works. Suppose you know 10 facts. Then you can come up with more than 10! (factorial) arrangements of facts from which to draw an original thought (any arrangement need not include all 10 facts). Suppose you know 100 facts; then there are more than 100! arrangements. The mere addition of 90 facts to a repository of ideas raises, in this example, the sample space for originality from large to astronomical levels.

The foundations of mind liberation through knowledge are words and numbers. Learning words not only permits one to understand reading materials (counteracts cognitive block) but also permits thoughts to appear that could not possibly appear in the absence of these symbols. "We have good grounds to believe . . . that thinking as we understand it is made possible only by the use of names or symbols" (Bronowski 1965:36). "Most people find it impossible to think without words" (Kasner and Newman 2000:2005). Thinking is obviously the fundamental part of creativity.

Having cached a large set of words in the appropriate depot, the scientist will find that using them to formalize thinking through writing might lead to creativity. Kaminer (1999:234) writes, in part, to discover what she thinks. Text is a verbal model of something, and therefore it helps to clarify and condense one's thinking (verbal descriptions and mathematical models are the only known methods of accomplishing these goals). Clarification and condensation through writing lead to the discovery of flaws and to the forced conjuring of more complete or more accurate ideas. Whether forced or free, conjuring is the same as creativity.

By study of numbers, I mean mathematics. Just as physical exercise adapts the body to physical exercise, mental exercise adapts the mind to mental exercise. Mathematics is cerebral calisthenics. The painful thought it invokes is practice for the painful thought invoked by attempts to understand and explain process in the field. Mathematics provides practice in conjuring up abstractions—x, for example—which might be viewed as something like a Poincaré hypothesis. Story problems in mathematics provide metaphors for the field (which is to some large degree a story problem). For example, when I studied differential equations, I encountered problems dealing with the spread of disease in England. These problems provided a metaphor for the spread of wariness in bobwhite populations through contact with hunters (Radomski and Guthery 2000).

Besides, equations and their ramifications are a type of language and thus set the stage for new thoughts in a manner similar to words: "Sometimes when you have a set of equations and you sit down with a pencil and paper, you find they contain more than you thought they did" (Silver 1998:95). In fact, insights derived from formulation and manipulation of equations are in a sense so easy to obtain that it feels almost like cheating, creatively speaking. Sometimes these insights are retrievable only by the formulation and manipulation of equations; that is, complex processes may be mentally tractable only in terms of equations used to describe the processes.

As Beveridge (1957:75) recommended, study (or at least recreational reading) should expand into areas related obliquely or not at all to one's bailiwick. A main reason for seeking creativity inside your field by going outside your field is that information within a discipline tends to become bound in iterations of consensus and tradition. You see the same old material repeated over and over; knowledge becomes mantra—mantra becomes knowledge. Exposure to out-of-discipline topics provides new ideas and approaches that may be applied within a discipline. The classic example in the annals of science is Charles Darwin's reading of Parson Malthus's *Essay on Population,* which provided Darwin a key construct (exponential population growth) for his theory of natural selection. For what it's worth, I got the idea of space-time as a unifying construct in the theory of habitat management (Guthery 1997) while reading Albert Einstein's (1961) lay-oriented exposition of special and general relativity.

What to read is a matter of personal preference. Certainly treatises on the philosophy of science are in order. Beveridge (1957) is an excellent, highly readable starting point because he puts science in succinct but general perspective. Other useful topics for natural resource scientists include popular physics for its elaboration of deductive science and principles of science, anthropology and human evolution, biology's role in history, and human behavior, among others. These general classes of knowledge put science and human influence thereon in grand perspective.

Finally, the mere doing of research may lead to creativity

through the acumen accumulated with experience and the chance of encountering unexpected results. "All the basic theories of modern science are essentially offshoots of new and unexpected results obtained in experiments" (Eigen and Winkler 1981:112). In field studies of sufficient duration, unexpected results almost always occur. Of course, results are unexpected because they are not in the repository of extant knowledge, or because they are inconsistent with extant knowledge. In either case, researchers might wonder how or why the unexpected results accrue, and the hypotheses they generate will be creative. Samuel Butler (1612–80) observed,

> All the inventions that the world contains,
> Were not by reason first found out, nor brains;
> But pass for theirs who had the luck to light
> Upon them by mistake or oversight.

Setting Up Epiphanies

An epiphany is a sudden, intuitive understanding of something (Eureka! response); it is possible to set up the circumstances for epiphanies to occur and to thereby suppress the inhibitory effects of knowledge and tribe allegiance. Inspiration and intuition often occur in reflective moments after a period of intense concentration on a problem (Beveridge 1957:72–108). It follows that creative scientists often experience protracted, painful thinking on an issue. They should also experience or schedule mindless activities such as gardening, walking, shaving, driving, fishing, traveling, jogging, woodworking, painting, and so on into their routines. These activities provide the reflective moments when the mind may work according to the graphical (if somewhat irreverent) process described by Robbins (2000:7; see epigraph). When the mind is not on the problem, the subconscious, the freewheeling neurons of Robbins, seem to go into a free-association dither with stored facts that leads to many bad ideas and some good ones. "[T]he subliminal [subconscious] self is in no way inferior to the conscious self," observed Poincaré (2000:2047); "it is not purely automatic; it is capable of discernment; it has tact, delicacy; it knows how to choose, to divine. What do I say? It knows better how to divine than the conscious self, since it succeeds where that has failed." The scientist has to strain the good ideas from the total set offered up by the subliminal self using thought and judgment.

Perspectives

Creativity occurs when an original thought is born. It fosters progress in natural resource science because without creativity, science would become an exercise in fine detail and false or incomplete knowledge would never be exposed. Knowledge, opinions, and beliefs occupying the mind inhibit the birth of new thoughts. Paradoxically, knowledge acquisition fosters original thought because it increases the number of possible thoughts. Learning words, studying mathematics, and reading out-of-specialty topics also foster creativity. Creative solutions to problems often occur during periods of relaxation following intense thought on a topic.

Above all else, scientific creativity comes from exercise of the human capacity to think. Releasing creativity is a difficult matter of unshackling established thought patterns through skepticism over and challenge of prevailing ideas. It is also a matter of seeing the obvious and trying to understand it.

Although creativity is needed, science might collapse willy-nilly if its practitioners became universally creative. Science needs a large contingent of foot soldiers who take other people's ideas to task. Ideas must stand up to challenge before they become a part of science's information base. Although the work could be described as noncreative, it certainly is important.

The young scientist also should recognize there is a potential downside to creativity. Science is conservative. It is skeptical of new ideas to the point of being violently opposed to them. Accordingly, young scientists need to pay heed to the traditional so that they build a record in publishing and grantsmanship. With that record (and possibly tenure) in hand, scientists have the security to broaden their work into novel and possibly risky areas.

Earlier I mentioned that when scientists tap their creative wellsprings, they need to strain bad ideas from the total set of ideas that are born. Critical thinking about these ideas, the subject of the next chapter, is helpful in identifying bad ideas.

CHAPTER 7 Critical Thinking

[Critical] thinking is always more or less troublesome because it involves
overcoming the inertia that inclines one to accept suggestions at their face value;
it involves willingness to endure a condition of mental unrest and disturbance.
—John Dewey (1910:13)

It is the property of true genius to disturb all settled ideas.
—Sister Mary Corita (source unknown)

I cannot see how there can be anything seriously wrong with [my theory]; but
then one never does see these faults until some new circumstance arises or some
ingenious person comes along to show how blind we have been.
—Sir Arthur Stanley Eddington (2000:1074)

We might define critical thinking as use of the mind to form thoughts
that analyze or judge the material in our knowledge base, including
the material we see in technical articles. Analyzing implies assessing
for logical consistency and freedom from bias, and judging implies
the act of drawing a personal conclusion on whether you accept the
information on offer as tentatively reliable, reject it, or reserve judgment till further evidence appears.

We practice critical thinking as one means of arriving at closer
approximations of truth. In a negative sense, critical thinking helps
identify those notions of truth that are inadequate or perhaps false.
In a positive sense, it helps in the generation of new ideas about
nature.

At this point in the book, you should have no problem seeing
the need for critical thinking in natural resource science. Forms of
reasoning (induction, deduction) may betray us in the field. The facts
we purport to traffic in often have traits that render them, at best,
provisional. Our sociality may literally blind us to impartial perception of reality. We tend to see what the group sees.

This chapter introduces critical thinking as a necessary process
for improving our knowledge base by testing prevailing ideas in the
laboratory of the mind. I introduce thought experiments and show
how they can be used in this capacity. I also introduce the technique
of thinking at extremes to test the generality of purported principles.
Finally, I provide a list of active practices you can execute to assist in
critical thinking.

Thought Experiments

Thought experiments have had enormous influence and importance in the sciences (J. Brown 2000:528). A classic and oft-mentioned thought experiment deals with Aristotle's premise that heavier objects fall faster than lighter ones, and that lighter objects act as a drag if attached to heavier objects (Sorenson 1992:61). Galileo imagined a big stone becoming attached to a small stone in the middle of their fall to Earth. Under Aristotle's premise, we should have an object that falls more rapidly because the combined object is heavier. But on the other hand, we should have an object that falls more slowly because of the drag effect of the smaller stone. Because we cannot have an object that falls more rapidly and more slowly, we are left with one conclusion: heavy and light objects fall at the same rate. The point is, as Galileo argued, the premise could be disproved by thought.

The work of Albert Einstein illustrates the use of pure thought in deriving astounding revelations about nature. His special and general theories of relativity were products of his mind, not empirical data. Skrabanek (2000) called Einstein the best armchair researcher we have ever had.

Thought experiments occur rather infrequently in natural resource science literature, but examples can be found. Romesburg (1981) provides one. He observed that Paul Errington first hypothesized the existence of a fixed threshold of security and later changed the hypothesis to a variable threshold. Under the fixed threshold, it is possible for harvest mortality to be 100% compensatory, that is, 0 animals lost from the breeding population for each 1 harvested, at least up to some threshold harvest rate. Romesburg thought, with the aid of mathematical concepts, about the implications of a variable threshold. He concluded that a variable threshold makes, "on average, 100% compensation between natural mortality and harvest an impossibility" (p. 302). Romesburg's thinking casts doubt on the assumption that harvest mortality may be, at least in theory, fully compensatory.

Another example comes from Guthery (2002:151), who questioned the dogmatic belief that greater interspersion of cover types was associated with increased abundance of bobwhites:

> Assume bobwhites require two cover types in some area
> and further assume that a point in the area is usable if it is
> ≤80 m . . . from the two types. Construct a checkerboard

pattern for the two types and gradually increase the size of the squares. When the alternating squares are small, all points will be usable under the definition as the size of squares increases. This means that as interspersion declines, bobwhite density remains constant. When the squares reach some certain size, the proportion of points usable will begin to decline, which identifies the limiting bound on interspersion. When the limiting bound is breached, usable space and bobwhite density will decline. Thus we will see situations where density increases as interspersion increases and where density remains constant as interspersion increases.

Leopold's (1933:132) law of dispersion (principle of edge) is a concept vulnerable to disproof by armchair reckoning. Yet the concept was elevated to the status of theorem because Leopold is an icon of wildlife conservation. This is an example of tribalism trumping critical thought.

Leopold stated that, given an animal with high type requirements and low mobility, its potential density (D) is proportional to the sum of type peripheries (S) in an area of interest. "High type requirements" apparently means the animal requires different types of habitat for daily and seasonal activities. The critical thinker sees immediately that, in a sense, Leopold defined edge-obligate animals and concluded they need edge. Leopold stated the law held only "within ordinary limits." We may express the law as

$D \propto S$, given ordinary limits,

where the symbol ($\propto$) means "is proportional to." Another way of stating the law is (Guthery and Bingham 1992)

$D = kS$, given ordinary limits,

where k is a constant of proportionality. Leopold did not explain what he meant by "ordinary limits."

A flaw is readily apparent in the model Leopold proposed. At the lower extreme for edge ($S = 0$), density is 0. But empirical experience indicates populations disappear before they run out of usable space (a population viability issue); Leopold would have added a negative intercept had he thought at the lower extreme.

Consider an edge-obligate animal that requires two cover types, woodland and prairie. Management decides to increase the

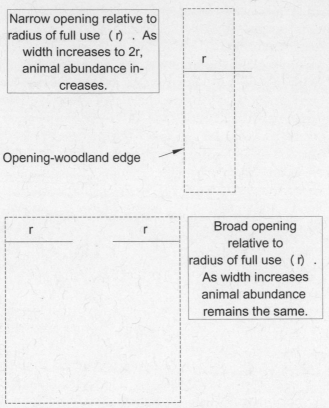

Fig. 7-1 Thought experiment for the principle of edge for a species that requires openings surrounded by woodland. *Top:* The quantity of edge remains constant, but abundance increases with width of the clearing. *Bottom:* The quantity of edge and absolute abundance remain constant as the width of clearing increases but density declines.

abundance of this animal by clearing openings in woodland (Fig. 7-1). Let us say the animal will venture no farther than distance *r* from woodland into prairie; it might use woodland for thermal and escape cover and prairie for feeding cover, for example. Define the length of the opening as *l* and the width as *w*. Then the area that a population of the animals may occupy (*A*) may be specified by the segmented function,

$$A = wl, \text{ if } w < 2r$$

or

$A = 2rl$, if $w > 2r$.

The top part of the function indicates the entire opening is usable because it is less than twice the distance (r) an animal will move from woodland into prairie. The bottom part merely states that the animal of interest will never occur farther than distance r from woodland cover, so when the width of the opening exceeds $2r$, portions of the opening will not be used.

If we ignore the effects of edge at the ends of the opening, the amount of edge along the sides of the opening remains constant at $2l$ as the width of the opening increases. However, the abundance of the animals increases as the area they may occupy increases, at least until $w > 2r$. In other words, abundance increases as the quantity of edge remains constant, and therefore potential density is not proportional to the sum of the type peripheries (Fig. 7-1). In fact, in this hypothetical situation, potential density is independent of the quantity of edge. This is a reasonable confutation of Leopold's "law."

Now we turn to a situation where it is possible to add or subtract edge from an area without changing the density of an edge-obligate animal (Guthery 1999b). We again invoke an animal that requires woodland and prairie habitat and that is subject to a radius of use r from woodland habitat. We deal with patches instead of blocks of woodland and prairie cover. Given the construct r, we find that within some minimum and maximum number of woodland patches, the quantity of woodland-prairie edge varies, but the area the population can occupy remains constant. This outcome explains the density-edge curve in Guthery and Bingham (1992:fig. 1). Likewise, the population remains constant because the area it can occupy remains constant. Therefore, potential density is *not* proportional to the sum of the type peripheries, and the law of dispersion fails again. This reasoning seems to exist well within ordinary limits.

It is possible to unravel the law of dispersion (almost literally) from other approaches. We first disprove that edge per se governs in a cause-effect manner (Leopold never said that it did; he said richness of edge vegetation and simultaneous access to cover types were cause-effect processes under the principle of edge. I argue below that richness of vegetation may or may not influence wildlife abundance.) Imagine a prairie lacking woodland patches. Add patches, and the abundance of our edge-obligate animal increases as edge increases.

Now suppose we unravel the patches of woodland cover until they are a few millimeters wide, and we spread this edge throughout the prairie. It is likely we will lose the population we created despite increasing the quantity of edge by several orders of magnitude. This outcome is consistent with theory presented by Guthery and Bingham (1992); that is, the density of an edge-obligate animal may decline as edge increases. Guthery, Green, et al. (2001) observed a negative relation between bobwhite density and the quantity of woody edge on farms and ranches in Oklahoma.

Or in an analogous manner, we can increase the quantity of edge on an area simply by changing the scale at which we measure edge. Mandelbrot (1983:25) has shown that the coast of Britain is infinitely long if the scale of measurement is fine enough. Also, analysis of the Koch snowflake, a fractal object (self-similar at different scales), reveals it is possible to put an infinite amount of edge on a 3 × 5 note card. Fine scales of measurement would lead to infinite sums of type peripheries in wildlife habitat. Leopold probably would say, and I agree, that the arguments in this paragraph take the question of edge in wildlife habitat beyond ordinary limits. Nonetheless, it is useful from a scientific standpoint to take a concept to its limits, for it is at the extremes that commonsense concepts are most likely to fail.

What does the critical thinking of Romesburg (1981) on Errington's threshold of security, Guthery (1997) on cover interspersion and the abundance of bobwhites, and the current example on failure of the principle of edge have in common? We have these common traits:

1. Start with a widely accepted if not dogmatic principle.
2. Decide to challenge the premise with thought.
3. Try to imagine plausible scenarios that would render the premise false.

If you are successful in the third step, then you have possibly done a valuable service for our knowledge base. Be warned! People might not be pleased with the result because dogma is comforting; many may be so enamored of dogma that they will not (and possibly cannot) see its faults, despite your lucid arguments. Admittedly, it is reasonable to harbor doubt over whether thinking alone can be trusted to refute presumed truths. A more complete refutation might require empirical experiments.

There would be more critical thinking if scientists took the second step (thoughtful challenge) more frequently. It is a difficult step to take, because we tend to become complacent over and develop belief in widely accepted "knowledge." We cannot, under these circumstances, even bring to consciousness the possibility that "knowledge" might be false.

Thinking at the Limits

Like portions of the edge example given above, the next two examples have the common property of thinking at limits, or extrema, of relationships to derive possible happenings in the in-between, where ecological events usually take place. This is a form of critical thinking about the relationship. Conjectural events at extrema, sometimes real, sometimes imaginary, help clarify the nature of hypothesized relationships.

The first example involves the simple assertion that abundance of some specified animal increases with plant species richness (loosely, diversity) in the area it occupies. This is a widespread— indeed, dogmatic—principle based on the premise that more diverse areas provide a more stable supply of commodities to animal populations as the environment varies. Here we think about how abundance (A) might change as plant diversity (D) ranges from zero to infinity, that is, the relationship $A = f(D)$. We can say some things about this relationship without collecting field data. We assume only that we are discussing an animal adapted to the area of consideration because, for example, plant diversity in the Amazon Basin is irrelevant to penguins.

We first consider low levels of plant diversity. Suppose plant diversity is 0 (no plants). Clearly, there will be no animals that require plants. Now think of a diversity of 1, 2, 3, 4, . . . species of plants. It is hard to imagine that an animal population can persist unless there exists some minimal level of plant diversity such that year-round food and cover needs are fulfilled. This implies abundance cannot possibly increase with diversity until the minimal level is exceeded.

Suppose diversity increases above the minimum level required for population existence. It seems reasonable to expect that average animal abundance will increase based on the premise that more diverse areas yield a more stable supply of food and cover commodities as the environment varies. Here we expect truth of the principle that abundance increases with diversity (Fig. 7-2). We do not know, how-

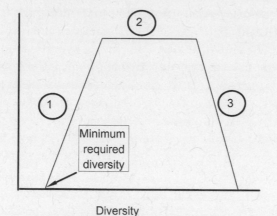

Fig. 7-2 Thought experiment for the response of a wildlife species to plant diversity. (1) After a minimum level of diversity is met, abundance increases with diversity. (2) At some point, increases in diversity do not increase abundance (abundance is independent of diversity). (3) When diversity reaches some exceptionally high level, it is imaginable that abundance declines with diversity.

ever, whether we might observe a gradually increasing abundance with diversity, which fits the premise, or a threshold effect, which fits in a different sense.

At some point, though, increasing diversity must have neutral effects on average abundance; that is, abundance will bear no relation to diversity. This will occur when diversity is great enough to neutralize all possible vagaries in the environment. Some other effect, for example, density dependence in survival and reproduction, will supersede the effect of increased diversity. Within a certain range of high diversity, the notion that abundance increases with diversity is false (Fig. 7-2).

Really stretching our imagination (indeed, going beyond Leopold's ordinary limits), we can imagine situations that are so diverse that the plants required by some target animal become rare in the explosion of diversity. This conceivably could lead to population declines (abundance declines with diversity).

What have we accomplished by thinking about the premise that abundance of some species increases with plant diversity? We have shown that, if it is true, it holds only within a certain range of diversity values. Outside this range, the premise does not hold. We have demonstrated the possibility that some researchers might report results in support of the premise, whereas others might report results refuting the premise—and it is possible for both reports to be accurate, at least if our armchair reckoning (Fig. 7-2) is valid.

The second example of thinking at the limits involves compensatory versus additive harvest mortality. The question of whether the recreational harvest of game animals is additive (population suppressive) or compensatory (population neutral) has long intrigued applied ecologists (since the 1930s, anyway). The additivity-compensation issue is fairly deep and definitely nuanced. That is, it involves a host of attendant issues, some less subtle, some more subtle, that our thought experiment dismisses.

Now the extrema that bound this issue are 0% harvest and 100% harvest. Clearly, 0% harvest is compensatory (has no effect on populations), whereas at 100% harvest, harvest is additive (eliminates populations). Am I going too fast? What is the nature of harvest mortality between these bounds?

Imagine low harvest rates as a percentage of the population: 0.001%, 0.1%, 1%, 2%, 3%, and so on. We know enough about the population dynamics of game animals to realize that such low harvest rates are inconsequential (compensatory).

Now imagine high harvest rates: 99.999%, 99.9%, 99%, 98%, 97%, and so on. Here again, our experience with and understanding of population dynamics indicates that harvest rates of this intensity will lead to the extinction of most, if not all, game populations, so these rates must be additive.

We have thus identified 2 domains of interest regarding harvest rates (Fig. 7-3). A certain low range of harvest rates is inconsequential, and therefore, harvest is compensatory within this domain. Conversely, a certain high range of harvest rates leads to population extinction, and harvest is additive within this domain.

In further analyzing the additivity-compensation issue from a swivel chair, we suppose that as harvest rate increases from low levels, it eventually reaches a level that breaches the capacity of a population to counterbalance harvest with density-dependent survival and production. Then the population must decline to extinction; time to extinction will depend on the degree of overharvest.

What have we learned if we accept the results of this thought experiment? First, the question, Is harvest mortality compensatory or additive? is ill-posed. It obviously is compensatory at low rates and additive at high rates. A more useful question is, At what rate does harvest become additive? Second, we suppose that in any popula-

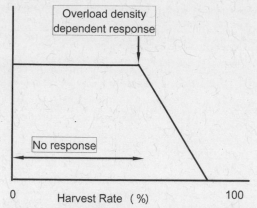

Fig. 7-3 Thought experiment on the nature of additive and compensatory mortality in game harvest management. Harvest is compensatory until the harvest rate breaches the capacity of the population to respond with density-dependent mechanisms.

tion subject to harvest that persists, harvest must be compensatory (although it is possible under logistic theory for sustainable harvest to reduce standing density). This is not at all surprising because we know predators have been exacting harvests on game populations for eons and that that harvest was compensatory. Death by talon, death by fang, and death by lead projectile have an equifinal outcome.

Active Practices

Here is a list of practices you can use to inspire critical thinking in yourself. The list undoubtedly is incomplete, but it contains some useful recommendations.

1. Read articles as if you were an anonymous referee. The editors of technical journals send submissions to reviewers who are known or presumed to have extensive knowledge on the topic of a manuscript. The purpose of a referee is to find fault with a submission and judge whether it is acceptable for publication (the editor makes the final decision). Finding fault involves examining the experimental design (if any) and methods for soundness; determining whether results are meaningful and conclusions drawn from them sound; and evaluating the submission as a lucid, crisp, unambiguous document.

The average reader of a published paper, on the other hand, tends to surf through the paper in search of facts of interest or pertinent to ongoing research. The reader seems to implicitly assume the facts are trustworthy, in part because the paper has passed muster in peer review; that assumption may often be false.

2. Reflect on what you have read or heard (think about it). Sometimes weaknesses or strengths do not reveal themselves in your mind until ideas have had quiet time to foment. Here is the approach of Leonard A. Brennan, Caesar Kleberg Wildlife Institute, Texas A&M University–Kingsville, concerning reflection as a part of manuscript review: "If there is a heartburn factor related to some aspect [of the paper] that seems troubling, I tend to sit on my [review] comments for a few days, even sleep on them, before I send a flamethrower. Sometimes I've mitigated my comments accordingly . . . other times, I've turned up the heat" (personal communication, 2006).

3. Watch for factors that might imply vested interest or bias on the part of authors, for these problems often imply a lack of full objectivity. Vested interest prevails when it is in the interest of authors to accrue findings that support their livelihoods or help to ensure continued funding from an agency, organization, or industry. For example, members of an agency established to control predators might be more likely to "find" (i.e., see) benefits of predator control in research results than persons wholly neutral on the issue. The problem is exacerbated if reviewers happen to be from the same agency. Doctors might be more likely to find therapeutic benefit from drugs if they are getting research funding from the company that manufactures the drugs (Skrabanek 2000:xxiv).

Word usage and rhetoric (argumentation) are other clues to potential bias (or lack thereof) in authors. Words may be euphemistic (something sounds better than it is), dysphemistic (something sounds worse than it is), or neutral. For example, humans might make love euphemistically, have intercourse objectively, or . . . well, you get the picture. We could call plants and animals from foreign shores "introduced species" or "alien species." We would take authors who used the former term as more dispassionate about the issue than authors who used the latter term. Sensitivity about vested interest and wording is a method of assessing the preconceived notions and mind-sets of authors and, accordingly, drawing inferences on how they might interpret and present the results of a study, and whether those interpretations are objective.

4. Include your own thoughts among those subject to critical thinking. You undoubtedly harbor opinions, values, and beliefs that render your thoughts vulnerable to bias. You have to think about whether the bias and shortcomings you perceive in the work of others reflect their problem or yours.

Critical Thinking in Life

Critical thinking is useful in life as well as science. A barrage of balderdash characterizes information flow at the start of the twenty-first century. The media, the politicians, and the special interest groups of all stripes broadcast ideas that range in quality from bloviation to biased perspective to baloney.

You even have to watch out for the do-gooders, as this quote from the Seretean Wellness Center at Oklahoma State University illustrates:

> *** Today's Tip: Processed Red Meat and Colorectal Cancer. A recent observational study of just over half-a-million European adults suggests that people limit red meat intake. While researchers aren't sure why the extra cancer developed, they found those who ate 5 to 6 ounces of red meat per day, as compared to those averaging less than 1 ounce per day, showed a 35% increase in colorectal cancer risk. The strongest link was to processed red meat. Chicken appeared to be neutral. Regularly eating fish, on the other hand, seemed to protect against colorectal cancer.

Critical examination of the statement reveals several possible flaws in the basis of the advice. First, with 500,000 subjects, the study probably was epidemiological. This means it was a search for correlations in a large data set, and we know that correlation might or might not imply cause and effect (chapter 2). Second, a "35% increase in colorectal cancer" is a relative number and might mean about anything. For example, an increase in colorectal cancer from 1/100,000 to 1.35/100,000 is a 35% increase but not especially meaningful in absolute terms. Third, should we be concerned about "red meat" or "processed red meat"? The wellness message is ambiguous on this issue. Finally, we observe that humans have been eating red meat for some few million years and, accordingly, their systems should be well adapted to the food.

Perspectives

The infrequency of thought experiments in natural resource science probably reflects, to some degree, unfamiliarity with the possibility of using such experiments to derive knowledge or challenge beliefs. Also, the community of natural resource scientists may have a culturally imposed bias against thought (including mathematics) as a font of knowledge; we tend to be strongly empirical. The bias, if it exists, also would suppress thought experimentation. Be that as it may, resource scientists practice informal thought experimentation when planning a study or sifting through alternative hypotheses. Certainly there is more room for formal, published thought experimentation in natural resource science.

Like induction, retroduction, and deduction, thought experimentation is a useful adjunct in science. Like these forms of reasoning, thought experimentation has pitfalls. For example, Galileo was wrong; we now have sophisticated measuring devices that disprove his conclusion that the rate of fall of objects is independent of mass (J. Brown 2000:198).

Nevertheless, it seems axiomatic that more thought is always better than less thought in the conduct of science. Scientific advancements start as thought; scientific impediments persist for lack of thought. Too often, we accept hypotheses or statements as fact when they may, upon critical review, reveal themselves as something not clearly fact. The most difficult mental act is the decision to challenge that which passes for sound knowledge.

At this point in the book, we have discussed aspects of natural resource science ranging from stalwart traditions to idiosyncrasies and opportunities imposed by the human condition. It is now time to turn to key aspects of the practice of science, beginning with a comparison and contrast of observational and experimental science.

Practice

CHAPTER 8

Observational versus Experimental
Science

> *Scientists have been studying [fluctuations and density limits in game] in the
> handmade glass-bottle environments of the laboratory. This is proper—they
> will some day extend their controlled experiments to the hills and fields. But the
> game manager faces it here and now.*
> —Aldo Leopold (1933:71)

> *Thus, the experimentalist utilizes the statistical analysis of his results to
> explain phenomena . . . , to predict future phenomena . . . , and thereby to
> provide a scientific basis for the prediction and control of phenomena. This is an
> exaggeratedly simple case, of course, for purposes of illustration to contrast the
> situation of the experimentalist with that of the mere observer who has little or
> no control over the phenomena he is studying.*
> —Margaret Jarman Hagood (1970:70)

> *It is hard to make sense of a cause being necessary for its effect in some universal
> fashion, because most effects can be brought about in a number of different
> ways.*
> —Paul Humphreys (2000:34)

This chapter begins with descriptions of the methodology in 2 studies that show contrasting approaches to knowledge accrual in natural
resource science. Cornaglia et al. (2005:36) "conducted experiments
under laboratory and greenhouse conditions to determine the effect of soil water content on seed germination and initial seedling
growth of Dallisgrass" (*Paspalum dilatatum*), including no stress (experimental control). They randomly assigned 4 replicates (50 seeds
each) to each of 5 water stress treatments. During the experiment,
they controlled evaporation with covers on petri dishes and exposed
replicates to a cycle of 16 hours daylight and 8 hours dark.

Schwartz and Hundertmark (1993:455) "quantified the estrous
cycle, estrous length, gestation length," and other characteristics of
moose (*Alces alces*) reproduction based on observations of the behavior of captive animals. To determine dates of conception, ovulation
rates, and calf production of wild moose, they extracted and analyzed
reproductive tracts of road-killed females. The size of fetuses provided
information on conception date, properties of the ovaries provided
information on ovulation rates, and the presence (or absence) and
number of fetuses provided information on calf production.

The 2 studies briefly reviewed above illustrate the 2 broad classes
of research in natural resource science: experimental (Cornaglia et al.

2005) and observational (Schwartz and Hundertmark 1993). Each class has a valuable place in knowledge accrual. The purpose of this chapter is to compare and contrast observational and experimental science by pointing out their differences and similarities. I also discuss their strengths and weaknesses and provide perspective on their roles in knowledge accrual.

Explanations and Examples

Experimental science is accomplished through experimental design such that the effects of extraneous variables are controlled for or neutralized and the effect of a variable of interest is tested. The experiment by Cornaglia et al. (2005) illustrates a high degree of control over experimental conditions. An extraneous variable is one that might influence a response but is not of interest in the experiment at hand.

The experimental approach usually involves analysis of variance (ANOVA) or one of its forms (e.g., the pooled *t*-test is a form of ANOVA). Hallmarks of the approach include use of an experimental control, randomization, and replication. Randomization ensures random errors, which in turn ensure the philosophical appropriateness of statistical tests. Replication is necessary to estimate variability so that statistical tests may be conducted.

In the practice of natural resource science, experimental research is used somewhat rarely to determine causes of an effect. It is used most often to estimate the magnitudes of effects for causes already known. The Cornaglia et al. (2005) research was a magnitude-of-effect study because there is no doubt that water is necessary for seed germination.

Determining causes is perhaps most useful when competing research hypotheses seem to explain an event equally well. As an example, the average body mass of midlatitude bobwhites increases from September to a peak in December and then declines to March (Hiller and Guthery 2004). This trend is negatively correlated with air temperature and day length, which are positively correlated with each other during September–March. To determine whether temperature or day length causes mass dynamics, the researcher would have to resort to controlled experimentation in the laboratory. Notice that in this example we have equally plausible hypotheses on cause, and we are experimenting on cause rather than magnitude of effect. This experimentation would involve studies with varying day length at constant temperatures and varying temperatures at constant day length. Whereas such studies might identify the most likely cause, given the hypotheses tested, the studies are not necessarily confirmatory. Other hypotheses simply not imagined might explain the effect.

Experimental science used to determine magnitudes of effects when causes are known (which is really descriptive, not experimental) follows the same protocols as experimental science used to determine causes. For example, an experiment might be conducted to determine the effects of protein levels in the diet on antler mass in cervids. An experimental design is created such that one or a few variables that might influence a response are varied while other variables that might influence a response (extraneous variables) are held constant or their effects are neutralized by randomization. In the antler mass example, researchers might apply treatment levels of 10%, 15%, and 20% protein in the diet. They might control for the effects of genetic propensity for large antlers by randomly assigning subjects to treatments. In theory, this assignment would cause the genetic effects to average out (the effect would average the same for subjects in all protein-level treatments, assuming no interaction between genetics and protein level). The researchers might also limit the experimental subjects to deer of fixed age to cancel out the effects of age on antler mass. All of these design elements assist in estimating the pure effects of protein in the diet on antler mass.

Observational science, on the other hand, characterizes research in anthropology, archaeology, paleontology, history, sociology, natural history, and field ecology, among other realms of research. Natural history involves observation and simple descriptive statistics on phenomena such as clutch size, litter size, diet, plant use, and so on. The Schwartz and Hundertmark (1993) study is illustrative. Henceforth, we exclude natural history from further discussion and focus on observational studies executed to elucidate relationships in nature.

A key difference between experimental and observational (relational) science is a priori, design-imposed control over extraneous factors in the former and lack of such control in the latter. However, a relational study might include in a model (e.g., regression, neural, logistic) information on the effects of extraneous variables on the dependent variable. Design elements appear in observational science, to be sure, but formal design-induced control does not. For example, a scientist determining the effects of food availability on average litter size in a canid would attempt to randomly sample a canid population and its food sources, but the scientist would have no control over these variables. The observational scientist might also include the effects of age on the dependent variable by including it in a model, whereas the experimental scientist might control for the effects of age, as the cervid nutrition example illustrates.

Similarities

If we view nature as a system of interacting parts, then we can abstract information about those interacting parts and the responses they engender in the form of mathematical models. We can use these models to predict the response of some variable of interest (e.g., animal demographics) as the interacting parts change in magnitude. We can compare observational and experimental science on simplified versions of this mathematical view of nature.

Comparative models from observational and experimental science might be expressed as follows:

observational: $y_i = a + bx_i + \varepsilon_i$,
experimental: $y_{ij} = \mu_i + \varepsilon_{ij}$.

The observational model represents simple linear regression, and the experimental model represents one-way analysis of variance (different levels of 1 treatment with all other sources of variation controlled or neutralized by randomization).

The first model states that "the value of the dependent variable, y_i, at a value of an independent variable, x_i, is equal to the y-intercept, a, plus a constant (b) times x_i plus random error of the ith observation, ε_i." The second model states that "the value of the dependent variable for observation j in treatment i (y_{ij}) is equal to the population mean of the ith treatment (μ_i) plus the random error associated with observation j in treatment i, ε_{ij}."

Now let us suppose x is a continuous variable. For example, x might range between 0 and 100, and μ_i might represent the mean of y at 3 arbitrary values of x_i, such as 0, 50, and 100; that is, we impose treatments of $x = 0$ (experimental control), $x = 50$, and $x = 100$.

We see based on the models given above that experimental and observational science are to some degree mere variations of the same idea. The prediction $a + bx_i$ of the observational model is a homo-

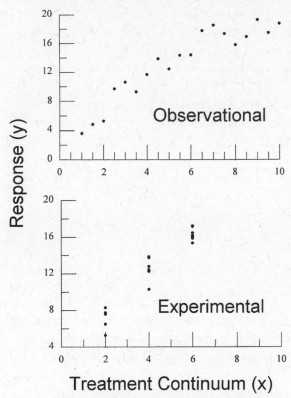

Treatment Continuum (x)

Fig. 8-1 Observational science may involve nonrepeated sampling all along a continuum, whereas experimental science may involve repeated sampling at fixed points along a continuum.

logue of the treatment population mean, μ_p in the experimental model. The major noticeable difference between the approaches is that we have repeated sampling at fixed values of the treatment with experimental, whereas we have sampling all along the continuum with observational (Fig. 8-1).

Let us suppose some variable, such as age of experimental subjects, had been controlled in the experimental model. Then we could posit an observational model of the form

$$y = f(x, age).$$

The above statement, expressed verbally, is "y is a function of x and *age*." Here we obtain a logical homologue for an experimental model that controls for the effects of *age*. Here again, experimental and observational models are similar.

Observational and experimental models are also similar in other ways, including their role in description and hypothesis testing:

* Both support magnitude-of-effect estimates.

* Both support hypothetico-deductive experimentation.

* Both support confirmation or refutation of existential hypotheses.

* Both require some degree of a priori planning, but experimental science requires more planning than observational science.

* Both may yield invalid results. No approach to science guarantees valid results.

Differences

The key difference between experimental and observational science, as mentioned above, is the level of control over the effects of extraneous variables in experimental science and either (1) no such control over or (2) parameterization of extraneous variables in observational science. "Parameterization" here means inclusion of additional independent variables in an observational model and quantification of the strength of that variable to predictions (e.g., a regression coefficient).

Further differences between experimental and observational science are somewhat philosophical. First, experimental science is regarded by many researchers as better than observational science. This opinion may obtain because the results of carefully controlled experiments are intuitively more likely to be valid than the results of experiments lacking careful control. However, careful control does not ensure valid results, and lack of control does not guarantee invalid results.

Second, observational science deals better with chain-of-events causes than does experimental science. A chain-of-events cause is the set of events that leads to an outcome. For example, a fawn-at-heel count in autumn is based on pregnancy rates and litter size in does and survival of fawns and adults from birth to the time of the count; survival rate is based on nutrition, predation rate, and random happenings. The events in a chain could be studied piecemeal (1 link at a time) with experimental science but are studied more efficiently and holistically with observational science.

Third, experimental science limits research subject matter. Not all valid research questions can be addressed in an experimental framework; indeed, many important questions are beyond the scope of experimental science. Obvious examples include large-scale studies of watershed treatments or the effects of landscape fragmentation on wildlife populations. Another example is the effects of harvest regulations on transnational waterfowl populations. At somewhat smaller scales (pasture, large study plot) it often is infeasible to sample sufficiently to legitimize the presumption that extraneous effects are averaged out by random assignment of treatments to areas. The sample size (number of replicates) is simply too small to meet the expectation.

Fourth, investigators who adhere to the experimental approach impose limits upon their imaginations, whereas observational scientists suffer no such imposition. Many researchers believe (belief shackles thought) that the only legitimate way to do research is under the framework of experimental science.

> We are trained to think that "hard science" models of quantification, experimentation, and replication are inherently superior and exclusively canonical, so that any other set of techniques can only pale by comparison. But historical science proceeds by reconstructing a set of contingent events, explaining in retrospect what could have been predicted beforehand. If the evidence be sufficient, the explanation can be as rigorous and confident as anything done in the realm of experimental science. (Gould 1993:77)

Belief in the superiority of experimental science limits imagination to questions that can be addressed under that framework. As I pointed out above, many important questions relevant to large scales must be addressed observationally. Also, the testing of broad-scale patterns might be impossible under an experimental framework because "treatments" are not the same across broad scales. For example, a "lower successional treatment" in Arizona is quite different from the same "treatment" in Florida. The point is that researchers enamored of experimental science cannot or do not try to conceive research questions or patterns not amenable to study in an experimental framework.

Fifth, there are legitimate questions about nature where experimental science need not be and possibly cannot be invoked. An example is the quantification of the estrous cycle, estrous period, and gestation period in moose (Schwartz and Hundertmark 1993). You see that the whole experimental framework does not fit in this example.

Perspectives

Experimental science occurs when it is possible to control (fix) and/ or account for, by randomization, all factors relative to a dependent variable. Observational science occurs when this (control, randomization) is not possible. Both approaches are variations of the same underlying idea, as illustrated by simple mathematical models of the two.

Neither experimental nor observational (relational) science provides a comfortable, holistic fit to all types of research problems encountered in natural resource science (Table 8-1), but each has advantages in special situations. In practice, experimental studies fit best in laboratories or pens where control over extraneous variables may be exercised. History teaches there may be danger in extrapolating the results of controlled studies to the field because findings in the field often are inconsistent with findings under controlled conditions; the reality of the field differs from the somewhat artificial reality of the laboratory or pen. On the other hand, many facts discovered under controlled experimentation extend readily to the field.

The reality of the field limits the application of experimental science. Occasionally there are feeble attempts (in the sense of sample size) to conduct large-scale projects in the framework of experimental science. Also, nature offers up natural treatments without experimental controls (e.g., sex, age, season, year) whose effects often are evaluated (somewhat gratuitously) under ANOVA protocols, although this practice may be philosophically illegitimate because treatments can neither be replicated nor randomly applied to experimental subjects (Hagood 1970).

Because achieving control over extraneous variables is difficult in the field, and because many important research questions are not amenable to experimental evaluation in the field (Table 8-1), it should not be surprising that the vast majority of field studies in natural resource science are observational. These range from descriptive natural history to habitat selection studies to relational studies involving models and model selection. The popular information-theoretic

Table 8-1 Comparisons between experimental and observational science

Comparison	Experimental	Observational
Controls extraneous variables or averages out their effects	Yes	No
Quantifies effects of extraneous variables	No	Maybe
Supports magnitude-of-effect estimates	Yes	Yes
Supports research on chain-of-events causes	Weakly	Yes
Supports confirmation or refutation of existential hypotheses	Yes	Yes
Supports hypothetico-deductive experimentation	Yes	Yes
Limits research subject matter	Yes	No
Limits investigators' imaginations	Yes	No
Applies readily to all field situations	No	Yes
Fosters purity in results (convincing results)	Probably	Maybe
Yields valid research results	Maybe	Maybe
Requires a priori planning	Much	Some

approaches to model selection (chapter 11) are largely observational (Guthery, Brennan, et al. 2005).

Whether one is practicing experimental or observational science, mathematics is an essential tool for planning studies, interpreting results, and forestalling logical blunders. We turn now to the role of mathematics in natural resource science.

CHAPTER 9

Mathematics

For really well-rounded work, [wildlife biologists] require the daily help of . . . mathematicians.
—Aldo Leopold (1933:418)

[T]he first difficulty the man in the street encounters when he is taught to think mathematically is that he must learn to look things much more squarely in the face; his belief in words must be shattered; he must learn to think more concretely.
—Hermann Weyl (2000:1834)

If you know a thing only qualitatively, you know it no more than vaguely. If you know it quantitatively—grasping some numerical measure that distinguishes it from an infinite number of other possibilities—you are beginning to know it deeply.
—Carl Sagan (1997:21)

A dilettante is a dabbler in art or knowledge. I admit to being a dilettante in mathematics. The dabbling started several years ago when my wife and I forced our daughter to take high school calculus. Oh, there was great moaning and gnashing of the teeth on her part. To appease my daughter, I agreed to work in unison with her, page for page, as she slogged through derivatives, integrals, and limits at infinity. My only previous exposure was a summer course called something like "Calculus for Dummies" at Texas A&M University.

She worked at the kitchen table; I worked at the card table in the back bedroom. As I studied, I began to feel like Oracle Jones in the movie *Texas across the River.* "I see it now!" he would shout as he sipped whiskey and conjured visions of the future. What I saw was the power of calculus in clarifying and explaining the mysteries of ecology.

Natural resource scientists do not, in general, seem to appreciate the power of mathematics in their science. The purpose of this chapter is to illustrate that power. Mathematical knowledge is necessary for (1) accurately transmitting information derived from statistical analysis and for comprehensive thinking on ecological processes, (2) enhancing the wherewithal of the analytical mind, (3) interpreting the results of statistical analysis, and (4) conceptualizing and manipulating thoughts to arrive at better or new understandings of nature. I address these topics in order.

Accuracy and Understanding

Strictly speaking, a faux pas is an embarrassing social blunder. I define it in this context as an embarrassing mathematical blunder in the society of natural resource scientists, which results in the publication and spread of misinformation. I am personally responsible for at least 3 mathematical blunders (Johnson and Guthery 1988; Guthery 1999b, 2002). These lapses involved miscalculations with equations that were appropriate.

Errors in mathematical syntax (the logical structure of equations) seem fairly common in natural resource science. Here is an anonymous example. "[T]he probability (p) of . . . was

$$\ln(p/1 - p) = -0.52 - 0.006x + 0.02y + 0.03z."$$

The authors have specified the natural logarithm of 0 ($p/1 - p = p - p = 0$) as a linear function of habitat variables (x, y, and z). The natural logarithm of 0 is constant at $-\infty$. The authors apparently were modeling the logarithm of the odds ratio, $\ln[p/(1 - p)]$ but made an error in mathematical syntax (failed to put parentheses below the dividing symbol). Moreover, the natural logarithm just defined is not a probability, but rather the logarithm of a ratio of probabilities. I have seen logistic regression models published in *The Journal of Wildlife Management* that had faulty syntax and, therefore, would never yield the correct prediction if applied by users who did not have the wherewithal to correct the syntax. Undoubtedly, there are many more examples in the natural resource literature.

In a somewhat related vein, failure to think mathematically about natural resource science issues may lead to the propagation and perpetuation of erroneous ideas. Leopold (1933:152–53), for example, described a line transect method of estimating ruffed grouse (*Bonasa umbellus*) density that was developed by a professor named King and came to be known as the King Method. The main problem in line transect estimation of animal density is the estimation of effective strip width (width of the area counted; you can measure the length). King walked along lines and measured the radial distance (shortest straight-line distance) between himself and a ruffed grouse when the bird was first encountered. In an arbitrary manner, he took the average radial distance to be an estimate of effective strip width.

The King Method, it turns out, has severe negative bias (Burnham et al. 1980). The bias arises because, for density estimation, the right-angle distance from the transect line to a counted object, not the radial distance from observer to object, provides the theoretical foundation for estimation of effective strip width. Indeed, the key feature in width estimation is an equation (detection function) describing the probability of detecting an object as a function of right-angle distance from the transect line.

The King Method probably was a product of an unchallenged "Eureka!" response—use the average radial distance for effective strip width—that not only bequeathed but also propagated biased methodology and blemished perception regarding wildlife densities. I do not know the courses on King's transcripts. But I wonder whether he might have been more circumspect about effective strip width if he had taken courses in trigonometry, probability, and calculus, or if he had visited a mathematician or statistician.

Today, line transect theory stands in quantitative elegance, primarily but not exclusively because of the biometrical work of Burnham et al. (1980) and Buckland et al. (1993). The theory is beyond the ken of natural resource scientists with no understanding of calculus. Effective strip width, for example, is the integral (area under the curve) of the detection function.

In fairness to Aldo Leopold and King, full appreciation of the general theory of transect sampling lay 40–50 years in the future. And in appreciation of them, they probably started biologists, statisticians, and mathematicians thinking about transect sampling; they introduced the concept.

Stanford (1972) provides an example of flawed interpretation of field results in the absence of mathematical mind-set. He constructed hatching distributions of bobwhites based on field sampling during the breeding season and based on backdating to time of hatch from wings collected during the hunting season. He discovered 2 peaks, an early one based on field sampling and a later one based on backdating; he took this as 2 pulses in production in support of his hypothesis of multiple brooding in bobwhites.

What Stanford failed to realize in accepting empirical results without mathematical thought was that his methods were guaranteed to give 2 hatching distributions, even if only 1 existed. Backdating favors the appearance of later-hatched broods because such broods have a shorter period to survive and therefore a higher probability of surviving to some time in the immediate future than early-hatched broods. Thus, backdating gives a biased image of hatching phenology—the peak appears later from backdating analysis than it is (Guthery and Kuvlesky 1998). We cannot completely forgive Stanford (1972) this misinterpretation because the backdating bias was reported in the bobwhite literature more than 2 decades before Stanford's work (Thompson and Kabat 1949). Stanford's flawed reasoning is interesting, however, because it supported the existence of multiple brooding in bobwhites when this common behavior was thought not to exist. He was right for the wrong reason (Guthery 2002:8).

The passage of time was Stanford's undoing; that passage perennially bedevils the pure empiricist who eschews mathematical reasoning. As an example, consider the seemingly straightforward matter of calculating the probability of nest success based on a sample of nests. The empiricist will simply find nests, divide the number successful by the total number in the sample, and let it go at that. The results obtained are likely to be wrong (Mayfield 1961).

Mayfield recognized that the passage of time invokes bias in nest success as estimated with the raw count data if nests are not found at the same stage of incubation. For example, a ground nest found on the last day of incubation may succeed with a probability of 0.95, whereas one found on the first day of incubation may succeed with probability 0.30. Mayfield recognized that the problem of time can be addressed by calculating daily survival rate and raising that rate to a power (the number of days of incubation) to obtain the estimated probability of nest success. For example, if the daily survival rate is 0.98, the estimated survival over a 23-day incubation period is $0.98^{23} = 0.63$.

Before Mayfield's paper, virtually all empirical estimates of nest success were wrong, and the ones that were correct (which we cannot identify) achieved this condition by accident of sampling. The biased estimates generated before Mayfield compromise the biological literature and will do so indefinitely.

Conceptual Benefits

Training in mathematics has at least 2 positive influences on the analytical mind: it fosters the ability to think at extremes and to think the arbitrary. Mathematicians have spent a good deal of effort in coming to understand the nature and even the existence of happenings at infinity. Likewise, the empirical biologist would do well to think at the extremes of practical issues, as we saw in chapter 7. Usually thinking at the extremes gives insight into the nature of the in-between, where practical issues arise. Many principles of wildlife management or ecology break down at the extremes and therefore tell us something about the in-between.

A difficult mental act is to formulate some arbitrary entity, such as a Poincaré hypothesis, as the basis for further argument. For example, below I discuss a probability-of-trampling model; the most difficult mental act in this model construction was defining an arbitrary construct, the base probability of trampling. After that definition appeared, the remainder of the model was a relatively straightforward exercise in basic probability.

Mathematics, especially proofs, provides good training in conjuring up arbitrary constructs: "Let $y = \ldots$" The variable y is a most general arbitrary construct.

Interpretation Benefits

A frequent approach to research is to collect data on a dependent variable and several independent variables and to search for statistical models that identify shape and strength of relationships between the dependent and independent variables. The analysis might entail simple linear, multiple, or logistic regression.

The first issue in this type of research often is construction of an explanatory model. In the 1-variable case, $y = f(x)$, the researcher needs to know how to apply polynomial, logarithmic, and exponential models, among others, to fit a straight line or curve. More complex curves such as the logistic or Gompertz might require that the biologist understand how to transform data and then detransform it to model data. This is run-of-the-mill mathematics that also can be applied to multivariable functions, $y = f(x_1, x_2, \ldots, x_n)$.

Model interpretation comes after model development, and interpretation requires knowledge of simple mathematics. The tendency of resource researchers is to quit interpreting the model when the "significant" independent variable(s) or the "Akaike best" model(s) have been identified (a possible reflection of inability in equation manipulation). This is unfortunate in part because variables in the models might imply significant or best-model nonsense (an effect deemed meaningful by statistical protocols that has no biological merit or is possibly ridiculous). On a more positive note, models often contain useful information derivable from model interpretation. Such interpretation might involve algebraic manipulation of a model or graphical analysis of the model's predictions.

With respect to model interpretation, the literature of natural resource science undoubtedly contains lodes of useful information that remain unextracted because natural resource scientists have not used mathematical pickaxes. The information is contained in graphics, tables, and equations, the latter sometimes generated by rote procedures such as polynomial regression.

Case (1972) provides an example. He studied the energy expenditure of laying bobwhites and reported that net food energy devoted to egg production (E; kcal/bird-day) could be approximated as a second-order polynomial function of operative temperature (T; °C) according to

$$E = -5.65 + 1.93T - 0.05T^2.$$

This equation suggests these facts: (1) energy devoted to egg production became 0.0 kcal/bird-day at temperatures of 3.2 °C and 36.1 °C, as determined by solving for the zeros with the quadratic formula; (2) net energy devoted to egg production maximized at about 19.3 °C, as determined by finding the first derivative of the polynomial and evaluating it at zero; and (3) net energy devoted to egg production declined at the constant rate of about 0.1 kcal/bird-day/°C at temperatures above 19.3 °C, as determined by interpreting the slope of the first derivative. These suggested facts were not reported in the paper; however, they bear on the field behavior of bobwhite populations under the heat hypothesis of reproduction variability (Guthery 1997). The maximizing temperature (19.3 °C) and the upper bound (36.1 °C) at which the Case (1972) bobwhites devoted all energy to survival and none to egg production are relatively low by field standards (Guthery, Land, et al. 2001).

The example of fact extraction from Case's paper is not meant or thought to be anything other than routine. It simply shows how mathematics (basic algebra and calculus, in this case) can be used to interpret models generated with statistical analysis of data. We will delve more deeply into model interpretation in chapters 12 and 13.

Further Benefits

The benefits of mathematics discussed above have positive implications on natural resource research, of course. The benefits that follow seem to me to have more direct benefits relative to our attempts to understand nature.

First, equations are a means of putting our thoughts on pattern and process into a symbol that is not only amenable to manipulation but also captures complexity with simplicity. An example follows.

Nest trampling by grazing cattle became a topical issue when single-herd, multipasture (short-duration) approaches to grazing began to replace old-fashioned continuous grazing (1 herd, 1 pasture) in the 1970s. Short-duration grazing was associated with extraordinarily high livestock densities on smaller pastures for short periods (e.g., 3–5 days). These high densities were properly alarming to conservationists concerned about ground-nesting birds.

The effects of short-duration grazing on nest trampling can be conceptualized with an equation that models probability of trampling. That probability depends on the number of livestock (h), number of smaller pastures over which the single herd is rotated (n), the time (T) required for the herd to complete a rotation through the n smaller pastures, and size of the whole area (A) containing the n smaller pastures (Guthery and Bingham 1996). The approach required that we define a base probability of trampling (q), based on 1 head of livestock grazing 1 ha for 1 day. This base probability is simply the proportion of an area trampled. The resulting model, subject to the constraints that livestock grazed randomly in space and nests were placed randomly in space was

$$P(\text{trampling} \mid h, A, T, n) = 1 - (1 - qn/A)^{hT/n}.$$

Although this equation appears daunting, it is based on simple laws of probability.

What does the equation imply? Holding time-based stocking rate (head-days/ha) constant but letting T (time for complete rotation) vary with n (the number of small pastures), if this equation is applied under different values for n, the probability of trampling remains approximately constant. What this means on the back forty is that a probability model predicts nest trampling is independent of herd rotation scheme, given stocking rate. Predictions of the theoretical model were consistent with preliminary empirical findings. Thus, the model gave an a priori indication of a pattern in nature.

The trampling equation per se is of no general consequence, except as an example of using mathematics to condense complex processes to a simple statement. Note also that we can solve the equation for any variable it contains. Thus, if we knew the base probability of trampling and the value of other variables in the equation, we could solve for the number of livestock (h). By extension to a wildlife research application, if we had an estimate of the base probability of a predator visiting a scent station, we could use the total probability of visiting scent stations to estimate the number of predators in an area. This is a value of being able to manipulate equations. It also is an example of deriving new estimators and new facts from equations.

The Lincoln-Petersen Index provides a classic example of the use of an equation to derive an estimator of population size. Suppose you mark and release M animals into a population of size N. Suppose further that you do a recapture after mark and release and you obtain m marked animals in a total sample of n animals (marked plus unmarked). If the marked animals randomly dispersed in the population, then the proportion marked in the population should equal the proportion marked in the recapture sample, that is,

$$M/N = m/n.$$

It follows algebraically that

$$N = Mn/m.$$

The Lincoln-Petersen Index, still legitimate if the assumption on random dispersion of marked animals holds, served as the progenitor of a suite of mark-recapture models in use today.

It probably is not too farfetched to say that any number derived from wildlife research could be considered the solution to some equation. Some numbers are easier to obtain than others. This opens up the possibility that, knowing an equation and having estimates of more easily measured variables it contains, we might be able to solve algebraically for some variable that is difficult to measure.

For example, the hatch-to-autumn survival rate of quail chicks has been difficult to estimate in the field. However, the autumn age ratio, clutch size, and adult survival—all relatively easy to estimate— contain information on the survival rate. By expressing the age ratio as a function of clutch size, adult survival, and chick survival in an equation, we can solve for chick survival and obtain an estimate without measuring chick survival per se (Lusk et al. 2005). Undoubtedly, there are manifold applications of mathematics in this sort of ecological sleuthing.

Finally, it is not possible to fully comprehend complex field processes without recourse to equations or sets of equations. The process of quail recruitment, for example, is complex and counterintuitive, and it is governed by events that take place after the fate of any particular set of nests is known. Quail renest (a future event in a chain), so the probability of nest success may underestimate the probability that any individual will recruit members into the autumn population. Because of renesting, recruitment is a nonlinear (and therefore counterintuitive) function of nest success. The increase in recruitment tapers off rapidly as the probability of nest success increases; extra recruitment is not particularly remarkable above 40% nest success and ignorable above 50%. (Bobwhites typically experience 30% nest success.) Success at a nest is relatively time consuming relative to failure (empirically determined); the practical ramification is that nest loss, in some sense, stimulates nesting activity and thus fosters recruitment. Nest depredation shifts the average nesting date to later in the season, which fosters observed recruitment (age ratio) because chicks hatched later have a higher probability of surviving to some future time than chicks hatched earlier (shorter time to survive). No amount of slogging about on the back forty is going to reveal the intricacies of quail recruitment. The proper insight is retrievable only with recourse to mathematical description (e.g., Guthery and Kuvlesky 1998; Guthery et al. 2000) of the relevant events in a production season. Undoubtedly, there are manifold analogs of the quail recruitment example in wildlife ecology.

Perspectives

Training in mathematics has 3 primary benefits for the natural resource scientist: (1) promotes accuracy in the transmission of quantitative information, (2) provides practice and experience in conceptualizing abstract events, and (3) yields biological insight leading to the development of new estimators and new information. It is not possible to fully understand complex biological processes without the aid of equations or sets of equations, for the equations are conceptual shorthand that may be viewed as a whole and manipulated.

Perhaps it is fitting to close this chapter with the observation that an icon of wildlife management and natural theology, Aldo Leopold, nearly got fired from his first job for shoddy ciphering (Meine 1988:92). But, as the first epigraph indicates, he came to realize a need for daily consultation between the mathematician and the field biologist. Leopold's (1933:418) recommendation of daily meetings is, of course, rhetorical. He must have come to realize, nonetheless, that natural resource science without mathematics is like business without balance statements.

A complete scientist of natural resources needs training in at least these courses: algebra to manipulate equations and handle calculus; calculus to understand functions and to handle derivatives, integrals, and limits at extremes; linear algebra to handle matrix mathematics; and probability with ample exposure to mathematical statistics to understand the probability models that undergird a great deal of natural resource research. Johnson et al. (2001) argued that a course or self-training in computer programming (e.g., Fortran, C, TrueBASIC) is beneficial because of the practice it gives in defining and solving problems, writing algorithms for process, and using the symbols of mathematics (as somewhat defiled by computerese). This amount of course work (18–21 hours) would not only improve the skill of natural resource scientists but also place vast quantities of quantitative tools and methods into the class, "that which is understandable and usable." For example, facility in mathematics much increases understanding of statistics and model selection, data analysis tools frequently applied without minimal or any comprehension of the logic involved in the tools. You will see the usefulness of mathematics in understanding the role of statistics, the topic of our next chapter.

CHAPTER 10

Statistics

> *When we reach a point where our statistical procedures are substitutes instead of aids to thought, and we are led to absurdities, then we must return to common sense.*
> —David Bakan (1970:251)

> *I have noticed . . . scientific studies that lacked thought and were dressed in quantitative trappings as compensation.*
> —H. Charles Romesburg (1981:307)

> *Our profession has become so smitten with statistical testing of 1 form or another . . . that science without statistical testing is almost inconceivable. In fact, science without statistics is unparalleled.*
> —Fred S. Guthery, Jeffrey J. Lusk, and Markus J. Peterson (2001:383)

Statistics as we know it today is a relative newcomer in the toolkit of scientists. It had origins in the work of Sir Ronald Fisher (1890–1962) of the United Kingdom, primarily in the 1920s and 1930s. He developed experimental design and statistical tests, among other contributions. Fisherian statistics so caught the fancy of scientists that these statistics came to be seen as almost obligate in the conduct of science.

Nowadays, graduate students in natural resource science frequently take at least 6 semester hours of statistics; some Ph.D. students minor in statistics. (I took 18 hours of statistics total on my M.S. and Ph.D. programs.) There is a major problem here. The training received by graduate students offers mainly rote analytical recipes and/or coaching in the language of statistical software. The statisticians giving this training, who are undoubtedly skilled in statistical analyses, generally have little empirical experience in the practice of science. Their only experience is peripheral as consultants to researchers.

What is missing from this training, then, is perspective. The purpose of this chapter is to provide perspective on the role of statistics in natural resource science. To properly appreciate that role, you must be aware of the misuses, abuses, and dangers of statistics. I discuss null hypothesis significance testing, which fell from grace in the 1970s or earlier yet is widely applied today. Finally, I provide some personal opinions on what your aspirations and values as an ecologist should (forgive me that word) be and how statistics fits into those goals.

Roles

Statistics may be viewed as rote mathematical recipes for abstracting information from or interpreting the meaning of data. Abstracting implies the derivation of a few mentally tractable numbers from a collection of data. For example, viewing 100 numbers in a matrix of data is not informative to the human mind. Accordingly, we abstract the numbers in the form of simple descriptive statistics. Examples include measures of central tendency (median, mode, mean) and measures of variability (range, standard deviation, standard error). The correlation coefficient (r), which indexes the strength of a linear relationship between 2 variables, is another example of a descriptive statistic.

Abstracting information from data may impose hidden burdens on the scientist. Consider the mean. "[T]he purpose of an average is *to represent a group of individual values* in a simple and concise manner so that the mind can get a quick understanding of the general size of the individuals in the group, undistracted by fortuitous and irrelevant variations. It is of the utmost importance to appreciate this fact that the average is to act as a *representative*. It follows that it is the acme of nonsense to go through all the rigmarole of the arithmetic to calculate the average of a set of figures which do not in some real sense constitute a single family" (Moroney 2000:1486; emphasis in original).

The mean per se has additional shortcomings because the process of abstracting might hide useful information. If a histogram of the frequency (count) of observations in classes (frequency distribution) is symmetrical about the mean, then the mean and median are the same and, hence, legitimate measures of central tendency. If, however, a frequency distribution is skewed (has a tail to the left or right), then the mean might be a questionable measure of central tendency. Certainly, the mean by itself gives no information on skewness; that information can be derived by constructing the frequency distribution and examining it.

Before turning to other forms of descriptive statistics, I want to mention a beautiful theorem of statistics, namely, the central limit theorem. If you were to repeatedly and randomly sample from a population, calculate the mean of each sample, and construct a frequency distribution of the means, you would discover that that frequency distribution is approximately normal. With a sufficiently large sample size, this result holds regardless of the nature of the frequency distribution of individuals in a population. That distribution could be skewed left, skewed right, uniform, bimodal, trimodal, or whatever. The distribution of means (i.e., the sampling distribution) will be approximately normal. Despite its possible shortcomings as an abstraction, the mean perhaps has more theoretical substance for the natural resource scientist than other constructs of statistics because of the central limit theorem.

Another form of description is the exploratory use of models to abstract information from a volume of data. A model may identify prevailing patterns in a data set (or it may yield nonsense, despite weighty statistical support). We rarely use the models we generate to make predictions about the future. Rather, we model to discover or quantify relations in a data set, and we then base knowledge on the relations so discovered, not the models. This is the way humans reduce complexity to something tractable to the human mind. We do not generally, for example, retain something like "y declined at a rate of 0.5 kg/ha with x." Rather, we simplify to "y declines as x increases" and catalogue this outcome in our repository of knowledge.

Statistical interpretation implies the use of statistical constructs to assist in judging whether the information in data is meaningful in the sense that it is unlikely to be a manifestation of chance. Interpreting implies the use of statistical tests, which in turn implies that probability is the basis of interpretation. We judge that the information in data is meaningful if the probability that it could have occurred by chance is low. Methods of interpreting data are essential simply because cost and/or scale make it impossible to sample enough so that we do not need the somewhat artificial prop of statistical testing. Given large samples, however, there would be no need for inferential statistics because all statistical tests would yield "significant" results. See Strickland and Demarais (2000) for an empirical example of all "significant" results associated with large samples. This outcome is further elaborated in the next section.

Bear in mind that inferential statistics is not a method of suspending human judgment, although some natural resource scientists seem to hold this opinion. Human judgment should not necessarily be trusted, to be sure, because of interpretation biases imposed by ego (Chamberlin 1890), existing knowledge (Dewey 1910), and tribe allegiance (Brothers 1997). Nonetheless, the application of statistical inference without judgment results in a sort of bingo science.

Indeed, it is impossible to conduct science on a purely impersonal basis (i.e., to rely on logical rules such as those used in statistical inference). Scientists decide what to study, whether to devote further resources to a research topic, and, in the final analysis, even whether to accept or reject hypotheses. "[A]s scientists learn their craft, they develop an ability to exercise scientific judgment which yields evaluations that are not carried out in accordance with rules, but that are more reliable than arbitrary choices. In addition, science is organized so as to marshal scientific judgment in a way that improves this reliability—although the element of fallibility is never eliminated" (H. Brown 2000:194).

Null Hypothesis Significance Testing

The null hypothesis significance testing (NHST) paradigm involves a null hypothesis, an alternative hypothesis, Type I and Type II errors, and *P*-values. The idea is to use estimates from sampling, variability of the estimates, and sample size to calculate a test statistic and determine whether means or other estimates differ in a probabilistic sense at some arbitrary level of probability. To understand how NHST is applied in research, we first define some terms.

Definitions

Null hypothesis. For present purposes, the null hypothesis is a conjecture that something has no effect on or is unrelated to something else; it is an existential hypothesis, as defined in chapter 2. For example, if we are interested in the effects of fat in the diet of an animal on its mass, the null hypothesis would be that "average mass is the same, regardless of the amount of fat in the diet" or, equivalently, "fat in the diet has no effect on animal mass." The null hypothesis is the basis for further analysis and interpretation.

Alternative hypothesis. For present purposes, the alternative hypothesis is a conjecture that something has an effect on or is related to something else. It is simply the negation of the null hypothesis.

Type I error. This occurs if a true null hypothesis is rejected. The probability of a Type I error is called the alpha level (α) of an experiment and is usually set at 0.05. At $\alpha = 0.05$, the probability of accepting a true null hypothesis is $1 - 0.05 = 0.95$.

Type II error. This occurs if a false null hypothesis is accepted (not rejected). The probability of a Type II error is called the beta level (β). The power of a statistical test is the probability of not committing

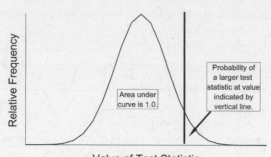

Value of Test Statistic

Fig. 10-1 Graphical illustration of the *P*-value.

a Type II error $(1 - \beta)$, which can also be viewed as the probability of accepting a true alternative hypothesis (i.e., the probability of rejecting the null hypothesis when the alternative is true).

Test statistic. This is a numerical index with an associated probability distribution (Fig. 10-1) on the basis of which we accept or reject the null hypothesis at the specified alpha level based on properties of a sample; familiar examples include the *t* and *F* statistics.

P-value. This is the theoretical probability of obtaining a larger test statistic (more extreme data, e.g., larger differences between or among means), given the null hypothesis is true (Johnson 1999), if the experiment were repeated infinitely many times. In other words, the *P*-value for any hypothesis is the alpha level at which the value of a test statistic is on the borderline between acceptance and rejection of a null hypothesis. The *P*-value is not any of the following: the probability the results were obtained by chance, a reflection of the reliability of the results, or the probability the null hypothesis is true.

We estimate the *P*-value based on the probability distribution of a test statistic such as *t*. The estimated probability distribution of a test statistic (Fig. 10-1) is derived from properties of a sample, that is, mean, variance, and sample size. We do not know that distribution; we estimate it from the data collected. We assume the distribution of the test statistic reflects what would happen if the experiment were replicated infinitely many times.

Application and Interpretation

Suppose we have a controlled, laboratory or pen experiment to test the effects of 10% and 20% fat in the diet on the mass of subject animals. We randomly assign subjects to treatments to neutralize extraneous factors. The null hypothesis is that, at the end of the experiment, animals receiving 10% fat will have the same mass as animals receiving 20% fat. The null hypothesis seems vacuous and probably wrong at the outset, but we proceed according to tradition.

We set the alpha level at 0.05. Why? This alpha level is completely arbitrary and wholly traditional; we could set the alpha level at any value we desire, but if we do not follow tradition, we might endure grief from thesis committees and referees and editors of journals. It might be unwise, from this perspective, to buck tradition. If we are concerned about accepting a false null hypothesis (Type II error), we could set the alpha level higher, for example, 0.2, since increasing alpha increases power if other conditions remain constant.

What does an alpha level of 0.05 imply? It implies we will *not* accept the null hypothesis if the probability of obtaining more extreme data is <0.05; that is, if $P < 0.05$. In other words, we will conclude we have observed a real effect. The alpha level (0.05) also implies the probability of obtaining less extreme data is 0.95.

Suppose we conduct the experiment and find the average mass of animals on 10% fat is 5.3 kg while the average mass on 20% fat is 5.7 kg, yielding a difference of 0.4 kg. The estimated $P = 0.1$. In this case we fail to reject the null hypothesis, given the alpha level we arbitrarily set. What does $P = 0.1$ mean? It means the probability of obtaining a larger test statistic (e.g., a larger difference between means) is estimated at 10% if we repeated the experiment infinitely many times. Alternatively, it means that the estimated probability of obtaining a less extreme outcome is 90% (100% − 10%). In other words, if you repeated the experiment infinitely many times, you would expect 90% of replications to have a smaller difference between means than that observed (0.4 kg). So you estimate that you would expect a smaller difference between means 90% of the time, but you are not willing to conclude that you have discovered a real effect of fat in the diet because you set the alpha level at 0.05. This outcome highlights the arbitrariness of the alpha level; you do not accept a 90% probability of less extreme data as meaningful, but you do accept a 95% probability as meaningful. Either probability is high; we would be delighted with 90% probability in gambling applications such as the stock market. Indeed, in gambling applications we would be delighted with a 51% probability of success.

Criticisms

The major theoretical criticism of NHST is that under the logic the null (no-difference) hypothesis is usually false: "The fact of the matter is that there is really no good reason to expect the null hypothesis to be true in any population" (Bakan 1970:235). The only reason that a no-difference null is not *always* rejected is that there is insufficient sampling. This can be illustrated with Student's *t*-test (Johnson 1999). Suppose we hypothesize that the mean in some population is 100. Then

$$t = \frac{(\bar{x} - 100)\sqrt{n-1}}{s}$$

where $\bar{x}$ = the mean of a sample, n = sample size, and s = the standard deviation of the sample. If we hold the mean and standard deviation constant, the t value increases with sample size and the P-value declines. The reason the t value increases with sample size is that the square root of $(n - 1)$ increases; remember, we hold the mean and standard deviation constant for this illustration. Suppose, for example, $\bar{x}$ = 100.1 and s = 10. With n = 100 we have t = 0.1; whereas with n = 1,000,000 we have t = 10.0; and with n = 1,000,000,000 we have t = 316. The point is, you can in general reject a null hypothesis with a sufficiently large sample size. If you can always reject a null hypothesis, of what value is such a hypothesis?

That a no-effect null hypothesis is almost always false does not mean there are no null effects in nature (Guthery, Lusk, et al. 2001). Nature is rife with what the rational scientist would deem null effects. For example, supplemental feeding of bobwhites seems to be a neutral (no-effect) practice. The virtually guaranteed falsity of the statistical null hypothesis versus the omnipresence of null effects in nature illustrates that the procedures, protocols, and theories of statistics often fail to fit the reality of nature.

Likewise, there is a large suite of problems in the application of NHST. These problems do not necessarily reflect deficiencies in logic, but they do indicate problems in application (problems ascribable to users). I simply enumerate several such problems.

1. Strictly speaking, certain forms of NHST hold for experimental studies but not observational ones. The reason is that randomization can be properly executed and extraneous factors controlled in experimental studies but not in observational studies.

In observational studies, we can attempt randomization, but we cannot guarantee it; we have no control over extraneous factors, and we cannot imagine repeating the study with extraneous factors that remained constant (e.g., weather changes). Lacking randomization, we cannot know the distribution of test statistics in observational studies (Anderson et al. 2000). Lacking knowledge of the distribution of a test statistic, we have no way of estimating P-values. This oversight in the application of NHST is frequent in ecology.

2. Besides almost always being false, the null hypothesis is mindless. However, some argue that the alternative hypothesis is a genuine research hypothesis (e.g., Johnson 1999) and that we state the null hypothesis merely as a formalism to assess the alternative hypothesis. In the diet example above, the null hypothesis is "there is no effect of fat in the diet on body mass." The alternative hypothesis is "there is some effect of fat in the diet on body mass." The alternative hypothesis remains mindless in this example.

3. Null hypothesis significance testing arbitrarily dichotomizes research results when research information is more properly viewed as evidence. Does it make sense to accept a null hypothesis at $P = 0.051$ and reject it at $P = 0.049$? "[T]he primary aim of a scientific experiment is not to precipitate decisions, but to make an appropriate adjustment in the degree to which one accepts, or believes, the hypothesis or hypotheses being tested" (Rozeboom 1970:221).

4. Researchers have confused the search for and presentation of statistical significance, that is, a $P < 0.05$, with the search for and presentation of useful ecological information. This has resulted in what is called the naked P-value, or the presentation of a P-value without any biological information (Anderson et al. 2000). Examples: "We found a significant effect ($P < 0.05$) on body mass," or "This variable was significant." Such statements are uninformative because readers do not know whether the effect was negative or positive, nor do they have any idea of its magnitude.

The problems of NHST have been known at least since the 1960s (Morrison and Henkel 1970). Johnson (1999) recapitulated these problems for the community of natural resource scientists. Yet in the early twenty-first century, you can pick up the most recent issue of any ecological journal and find articles that are rife with null hypotheses and P-values. "The statistical null hypotheses testing paradigm has become so catholic and ritualized as to seemingly impede clear thinking and alternative analysis approaches" (Anderson et al. 2001:315). What is going on?

Johnson (1999:767) listed several hypotheses on why statistical hypothesis testing is so prevalent:

> Such tests appear to be objective and exact.
>
> The tests are readily available and easily invoked in statistical software packages.
>
> Students and scientists are taught to use them.
>
> Some journal editors and thesis advisors demand them.
>
> Everybody else seems to use statistical tests.

Note that "statistical tests assist in finding reliable knowledge" is conspicuous by its absence in this list.

The continued application (everybody seems to do it) of NHST probably has other explanations that start with the advent of statistical analyses. As we discussed earlier in chapter 5, humans are by nature tribe allegiant, so when some scientists started using NHST early on, others followed suit and the movement gained momentum. The community of scientists came to view NHST as the "right" thing to do; this "righteousness" was enforced in peer review and editing. In this sense, NHST became a sort of faith-based approach to doing research. The point is, faith-based behaviors tend to linger in mind and practice; they are hard to release.

Finally, some biologists argue that, under certain conditions, NHST has a legitimate place in natural resource science (Stephens et al. 2005). If this argument is accurate, the algorithm might appear in ecological journals into the indefinite future. I tend to agree with Stephens et al. When there are simple dichotomous situations—effect versus no effect, relation versus no relation—the P-values associated with NHST provide a *descriptive statistic* that summarizes the information contained in samples relative to the dichotomous property of interest. The P-index takes into account magnitude of difference, uncertainty, and sample size and helps the scientist *judge* whether results are noteworthy. Of course, in many dichotomous situations, effects are known and the relevant issue is their magnitudes. Here NHST is gratuitous.

Misuses and Dangers

The body of knowledge encompassed by statistics, including NHST, is harmlessly pure and innocent in the same sense as a rock. The misuses and dangers associated with statistics reside in the minds and practices of its users. The problems include overapplication of imaginary statistical concepts in real-world situations, underinterpretation of statistical results, and overappreciation of statistical results.

Overapplication appears in 2 forms. The first is the notion that the rules, assumptions, or protocols of statistics must be applied to interpret nature. This false assumption inhibits scientific creativity by confining thought to that which is sanctioned in the artificial world of statistics. Consider, for example, the rule (assumption) of homogeneous variance (homoscedasticity) for the y-variable in a regression. The only reason for this assumption is the conduct of statistical tests on the parameters in a model. This artificial statistical rule does not prevent one from fitting a least squares regression line to data that violate the assumption to derive an estimate of the linear relation between y and x. This might be useful for descriptive purposes, regardless of whether statistical tests on the parameters are legitimate. Besides, the existence of heteroscedasticity is of scientific interest. Why does it occur? What can be learned from it? Heteroscedasticity might be an observation begging for a retroductive hypothesis on how or why. There might be, in general, something of scientific interest whenever data fail to fit a statistical rule. But the natural resource scientist imbued with artificial statistical rules would probably ignore the more interesting phenomena (e.g., heteroscedasticity) and conduct some transformation on y to fit a statistical assumption. Keep in mind that when data from nature violate a statistical assumption, we have a problem with statistics, not nature.

Another example of a different kind of overapplication is the seemingly prevailing notion that statistics is necessary for "good science." This notion is easily falsified because none of the major scientific accomplishments of Western civilization relied on or even used statistics. Examples include the work of Gregor Mendel, Sir Isaac Newton, Albert Einstein, and Charles Darwin.

Regarding underinterpretation of statistical results, natural resource scientists do not seem to explore their meaning or biological implications. Interpretation seems to slow or stop when a "significant" result is identified. The high prevalence of naked P-values in the ecological literature (Anderson et al. 2000) provides an example of this behavior. In purely inferential statistics, a "significant" result might be biologically meaningless, especially given large samples, which come to virtually guarantee all results are "significant" (a result of such results may be "significant" nonsense). It is up to authors to ask themselves and explain to readers whether "significant" statistical outcomes have any biological substance.

Relative to these ideas, it is important to realize that the use of statistics does not necessarily imply rigor. To a large degree, that use implies adherence to social imperatives in the community of referees and editors. It also might imply pretension (trying to impress with your knowledge) or obfuscation (trying to camouflage weak results with statistical mumbo-jumbo). Accordingly, many published articles contain unnecessary statistical folderol (a low ratio of biology to statistics) when descriptive simplicity could have prevailed. Simplicity facilitates the transfer of information from authors to readers.

This brings us to the danger of giving more credence to statistical results than they deserve. When we accept any statistical result, we implicitly assume the data upon which the result is based were of acceptable quality, implying the data were representative of the state of nature at the time they were collected. This is a troubling assumption in field ecology, especially with small samples. In human medicine, the results of any 1 study are viewed as provisional until the study is replicated in the scientific sense (i.e., repeated by different scientists or on new subjects; Sackett et al. 2000). This is a means of guarding against chance idiosyncrasies in the original data set. Scientific replication, or at least the collection and analysis of validation data, is largely absent in natural resource science.

Ecology versus Statistics

From the standpoint of human aspirations, we seek reliable knowledge about nature. Statistics is a possible aid in the acquisition of reliable knowledge and no more; it is a means, not an end (Guthery, Lusk, et al. 2001). It is subservient to ecology because ecological ideas, not statistics, drive natural resource science. For example, Darwin's idea of natural selection is arguably the greatest idea ever to enter biological thought. Other ideas of more recent vintage include source-sink populations, fragmentation, edge effects, genetic drift, niche gestalt, ecological succession, trophy buck management, usable space, and the handicap principle. These are ecological, not statistical, ideas; and such ideas, not statistics, are the measure of ecologists.

Here are some practical recommendations for placing statistics and ecology in perspective:

1. Remember that you are an ecologist. Remember that statistics is only a tool, that it might be misleading, and that it does not suspend the need for human judgment. "No inferential approach has an innate 'understanding' of biology; this is where the researcher's own judgement [*sic*] is crucially important, regardless of the approach used" (Stephens et al. 2006:195). This quote holds for model selection, the subject of the next chapter.

2. Put biological information and understanding on top of your priority list; put statistical analysis on the bottom. Recognize that statistical testing is a sort of crutch we use because we cannot sample sufficiently because of expense and time.

3. Put at your disposal the full panoply of analytical methods, including nonstatistical ones. This panoply includes logical argument, effect size estimation, graphical analysis, qualitative analysis (Guthery, Lusk, et al. 2001), repeatability of results, and model selection (Johnson and Omland 2004), among others. *On the Origin of Species* is a gathering of facts from which logical arguments ensue; it contains no statistical tests.

4. If you are doing a magnitude-of-effect study, state this at the outset. Such straightforward studies need not be encumbered with statistical folderol other than descriptive statistics and confidence limits.

5. Minimize use of statistics in your writing to the maximum extent possible. Many statistical tests (with P-values) reported nowadays are gratuitous, and this reporting encumbers and obfuscates papers. Gratuitous statistical tests come in at least 2 versions. One is the reporting of a P-value when it is obvious, by inspection, that a difference does not exist. "The means (± 1 SE) were 11.2 ± 0.5 and 11.3 ± 0.6 ($P > 0.05$)." The second version occurs when the null hypothesis is—if this is possible—even more vacuous than usual. Questions like, Did abundance differ between years? are obviously answered in the affirmative. We do not need statistical tests to draw a conclusion. Remember that it is not imperative that a paper even contain statistical tests. As mentioned above, eliminating unneces-

sary statistical posturing will result in papers that are easier to read and understand.

Perspectives

The primary roles of statistics in natural resource science are to abstract information from data, find patterns in data, and conduct tests to help researchers judge the meaningfulness of results. It should be kept in mind that the concepts, assumptions, and rules of statistics are wholly artificial relative to events in nature. That is, events and processes in nature operate independent of any concepts in statistics. Null hypothesis significance testing, though still widely applied in the early twenty-first century, is problematic in that null hypotheses are a priori false, in general, and statistical tests often are applied to questions with obvious answers.

Given the foregoing discussion, one might wonder whether the benefits of statistics outweigh its dangers in natural resource science. Again, statistics is but a neutral collection of abstract concepts. Benefits and dangers are products of human application of the concepts. The community of natural resource scientists has, by and large, become ritualistic about statistics; the community has exalted method over knowledge accrual. I think the situation is well summed up by Anderson et al. (2001:315): "The statistical null hypotheses testing paradigm has become so catholic and ritualized as to seemingly impede clear thinking and alternative analysis approaches."

One alternative to the NHST paradigm has recently insinuated itself upon the community of natural resource scientists. It is called model selection; it eliminates statistical tests per se but retains a numerical, decision-support index called the Akaike Information Criterion. We discuss the pros and cons of model selection in the next chapter.

CHAPTER 11

Model Selection

We recommend the information-theoretic approach for the analysis of data from observational studies. In this broad class of studies, we find that all the various hypothesis-testing approaches have no theoretical justification and may often perform poorly.
—Kenneth P. Burnham and David R. Anderson (2002:vii)

[The protocols of model selection] are all matters of opinion on which conscientious statisticians and users of statistics can legitimately disagree without making a provable logical error.
—Joseph B. Kadane and Nicole A. Lazar (2004:286)

We question whether the growing popularity of model selection based on information theory . . . and using the Akaike's Information Criterion . . . [represents] a useful paradigm shift in data analysis or a substitution of 1 statistical ritual for another.
—Fred S. Guthery, Leonard A. Brennan, Markus J. Peterson, and Jeffrey J. Lusk (2005:457)

The idea of selecting a best or a small set of better statistical models from a set of candidate models has been around for some time. For example, there have long been forward and backward selection algorithms for regression models.

With the appearance of Burnham and Anderson's (1998) book on information-theoretic model selection, the community of wildlife scientists became caught up in a stampede to apply this new approach to data analysis (Guthery, Brennan, et al. 2005). Other natural resource sciences have been slower to adopt model selection tools, but these tools are making inroads outside wildlife science. Surely model selection will become more prevalent in the ecological sciences as time passes.

This chapter gives a simple introduction to model selection using the Akaike Information Criterion (AIC). It starts with an explanation of the criterion, discusses model construction, and provides examples of model selection under logistic regression and polynomial models. Finally, it discusses when to use model selection in natural resource science.

Akaike Information Criterion

The AIC is a statistic that assists the researcher in finding so-called optimal trade-off between bias (model too simple) and variance (model too complex). It is intuitive that a simple model used to describe a complex system might be biased in the sense that its predictions miss the mark in a consistent fashion. When variables are added to a model, however, uncertainty of prediction increases because of the addition of more estimated parameters. So bias declines with the addition of variables to a model, but at the same time variance increases; as variance increases, confidence limits broaden until, at some point, predictions contain so much uncertainty that they are worthless. The AIC helps in identifying models that simultaneously minimize bias and variance.

Note that this rationale (minimizing bias and variance) may have little to do with biological reality; it is a statistical concept. The rationale is no less arbitrary than a *P*-value in statistical testing. Moreover, satisfying the rationale might imply nothing about the merit of a model with respect to the reality of processes in the field.

The AIC is given as (Burnham and Anderson 2002)

$$\text{AIC} = -2 \ln[\ell(\hat{\theta}|\text{data})] + 2K,$$

where

ln = the natural logarithm of the quantity in parentheses (the logarithm to the base e = 2.718).

$\ell(\hat{\theta}|\text{data})$ = the likelihood, or joint probability, of the parameters ($\hat{\theta}$) in the model, and the vertical slash implies "given the data from which the parameters were estimated." As an example, the likelihood or joint probability of obtaining 2 consecutive heads on 2 flips of a coin is (0.5)(0.5) = 0.25. The log-likelihood is ln(0.25) = −1.386. Parameters are numbers such as intercepts and coefficients.

K = the number of estimable parameters in a model. For example, in a simple linear regression model, $y = a + bx$, there are 3 estimable parameters: the intercept a, the slope b, and the variance (s^2).

Statistical software packages usually provide an estimate of the log-likelihood of the parameter set ($\hat{\theta}$) in a model.

The above definition of AIC is for large samples (n). In the small-sample case ($n/K < 40$), use the following:

$$\text{AIC}_c = -2\ln[\ell(\hat{\theta}|\text{data})] + 2K + \frac{2K(K+1)}{n-K+1}.$$

You are always safe using AIC$_c$ because the third term disappears as n grows larger and larger. That is, AIC$_c$ converges on AIC as sample size increases.

Model Development

The first step in model development is to become familiar with what is known about the subject of study. What are the commonsense relationships? Have other researchers developed related models that provide some guidance in model construction? Is there general knowledge of what variables should be included in a model that predicts the response of interest? Are there obvious (trivial) factors that should be in a model, such as year effects on the survival of *r*-selected species? Familiarity grows with thinking and with time spent reading the literature.

The second step is to posit a global or most complex model (largest number of parameters, K). The global model contains all the variables—and no more—that might reasonably, logically, and biologically be expected to influence the dependent variable. Here are some guidelines in selecting variables for the global model.

1. Select independent variables with obvious effects (and do not be surprised if they appear in a selected model). An example is year or area effects on annual survival rates; there remains no question that survival of animals differs among years and areas. The reason to put these effects in, even though they may be trivial, is to obtain a model that predicts well. Given such a model, it is possible to more precisely explore the biological meaning of other independent variables because the trivial effect explains variation.

2. Select independent variables for which effects have been reported in the literature. In general, it is wise to test previous findings on independent data. Select independent variables for which you have evidence (unpublished data, biological reasoning) of effects on the dependent variable. Perhaps you have done a pilot study to assess the merit of potential variables. Biological reasoning involves the use of natural history information. For example, if we know from descriptive natural history that better-concealed nests experience higher survival rates, and if we were developing a model to predict nest success, then we might put some variable such as percentage of visual screening of a nest in the global model.

3. Select independent variables not correlated with each other. Correlated variables in models sometimes lead to biological nonsense, especially in multiple regression applications (we will see an example in chapter 13). To determine whether you have correlated variables, you could simply generate and examine a matrix of correlation coefficients. You can also identify linearly correlated variables with factor or principle component analysis. These tools help to identify groups of correlated variables that are not correlated with other groups of correlated variables. They essentially summarize the patterns in a matrix of correlation coefficients. You might select 1 variable that makes biological sense from each set of intercorrelated variables.

The third step is to parse the global model into a set of smaller (fewer parameters) models that make sense based on knowledge and thought. For example, you might expect a weak effect of some independent variables that could be removed. You might want to test models without interaction terms. You would certainly want to test simple models that you expect to be explanatory or predictive. Some statisticians argue that these smaller models should be nested in the global model. This means that any term that appears in a smaller model should be in the global model. For example, $y = a + bx$ is nested in $y = a + bx + cx^2$, but $y = a + dx$ is not nested in the second equation because the second equation does not contain the coefficient d.

One has to be careful about creating submodels from the global model because there may be hundreds or thousands to choose from. Suppose, for example, that a global model contains 10 variables. Then there are $2^{10} - 2 = 1{,}022$ submodels consisting of 1 or 2 or 3 or . . . or 9 variables.

The possibility of placing interaction terms and variable transformations in the global model increases the number of possible submodels. Consider 3 variables, x_1, x_2, and x_3, which yield 4 potential interaction terms $(x_1 x_2, x_1 x_3, x_2 x_3, x_1 x_2 x_3)$. The researcher might decide to include quadratic terms for the x variables (x_1^2, x_2^2, x_3^2) to account for curvilinear trends in the data. Thus, 3 modeling entities (the x_i) grow to a total of 10, and the number of possible submodels grows accordingly.

"Every attempt should be made to keep the number of candidate models small" (Burnham and Anderson 2002:441). The best way I know of to keep that number small is to avoid guesswork altogether. Model selection has ushered in an era of guess-based science. You rarely see biological or logical rationales for constructing and splitting a global model. Two-way interaction terms frequently appear in candidate models, and I suspect many of these are outright guesses. Inclusion of 3-way interaction terms are almost certainly guesses because 3-way interactions are essentially beyond human comprehension. If you can provide a rationale for each model in the candidate set, you are not guessing.

Interpretation of Analyses

Because AIC is a relative measure of model quality, you must first determine whether the global model is meritorious in a predictive sense. You *will* find an Akaike best model, even if all of the models evaluated are outrageously bad. You can evaluate the global model in a predictive sense with traditional statistics, such as R^2 (proportion of total variance explained by the model) in multiple linear regression. For logistic regression, you can estimate R^2 or determine the accuracy of predictions in binary (0, 1) situations. If the global model is not useful in this predictive sense, there is no point in proceeding further. *You have nothing.* You have to decide for yourself whether you have *something;* there are no statistical crutches to support your decision. If the global model is meritorious, then more parsimonious (fewer parameters) models may be acceptable. You probably should test the more parsimonious models to determine whether they are meritorious in the predictive sense, just to be safe.

Given an acceptable global model, the Akaike best model, which may not be the best model or even a good model, is identified as the one with the smallest AIC value (AIC_{min}). Other models can be compared to the best model by calculating

$$\Delta AIC_i = AIC_i - AIC_{min}.$$

Models (*i*) with $\Delta AIC_i < 2$ are said to be plausible; plausible models deserve cautious interpretation. Such models might be valid, or they might imply the addition of a junk variable that maintains $\Delta AIC_i < 2$ (Guthery, Brennan, et al. 2005). The AIC algorithm has a tendency to overparameterize (select unnecessary independent variables; Kadane and Lazar 2004).

Logistic Regression Example

This example relates to a logistic regression equation for predicting the presence or absence of calling male bobwhites on 50-ha plots in the Ouachita National Forest, Arkansas. The example also shows how model selection can be used to test alternative hypotheses, in this case edge versus usable space, as explanations of bobwhite abundance. The dependent variable was presence (1) or absence (0). The independent variables were

u = usable space (suitable permanent cover; ha) in the 50-ha plots,
d = Shannon diversity of cover types in the 50-ha plots, and
e = Shannon evenness of cover types in the 50-ha plots.

Shannon diversity and Shannon evenness were not correlated with each other based on factor analysis. The global model consisted of all 3 independent variables {u, d, e}; that is, we use all 3 variables in developing a logistic regression equation to predict the presence or absence of calling bobwhites:

presence = *function of* (usable space, diversity, evenness).

It was partitioned into the following smaller models: {u, d}, {u, e}, {d, e}, {u}, {d}, and {e}. The models may be expressed verbally as

presence = *function of* (usable space, diversity),
presence = *function of* (usable space, evenness),

.

.

.

presence = *function of* (evenness).

Note that the smaller models are nested in the global model in this example. The partitioning was done arbitrarily in an exploratory sense. All of the independent variables might have been predictive based on a priori knowledge. However, there was no compelling reason for advancing the pared models other than to test models for the comparative performance of edge and usable space as predictors. The analysis was done on SYSTAT, which provided log-likelihoods; the other terms in AIC_c were calculated by hand.

The global model predicted presence or absence with an accuracy of 61% (checking the predictive value of the model; Table 11-1). This was a relatively low rate and implies the model was a weak pre-

Table 11-1 Evaluation of logistic regression models for predicting the presence or absence of calling male bobwhites, Ouachita National Forest, Scott County, Arkansas

Variables in model	K	AIC_c	ΔAIC_c	Proportion correct
u, d, e^a	4	100.4	0.50	0.61
u, d	3	100.7	0.80	0.59
u, e	3	101.2	1.34	0.59
d, e	3	110.7	10.81	0.54
u	2	99.9	0.00	0.59
d	2	109.3	9.44	0.54
e	2	109.8	9.98	0.53

Note: Data were collected in 2000 and 2001 on 50-ha, circular plots ($n = 80$).
[a]u = usable space (ha), d = Shannon diversity, e = Shannon evenness.

dictor of presence (a flip of the coin would yield 50% accuracy). However, I will continue for illustrative purpose. The Akaike best model (AIC_{min}) had usable space (u) as the sole predicting variable. However, any model that contained usable space was plausible ($\Delta AIC_i < 2$). This could be an example of the ΔAIC criterion including junk variables (overparameterizing), to which researchers must be sensitive. Use of landscape metrics (diversity, evenness) resulted in implausible models ($\Delta AIC_i > 9$). Usable space appeared to perform better than edge as a predictor.

Polynomial Regression Example
Model selection using information-theoretic protocols is particularly easy with least squares regression models. The information criterion is

$$AIC_c = n \ln(s^2) + 2K + \frac{2K(K+1)}{n-K-1}$$

where

$$s^2 = \frac{SSR}{n} = \frac{\sum (y_i - \hat{y})^2}{n}$$

The data used to illustrate model selection with regression are quail hunting records from the state of Arizona. The dependent variable (y) is hunter skill, defined as harvest/(bird in the population)/(hunter-day). The independent variable (x) is an index of quail abundance in the state. The sample size is $n = 18$. We want to select the best model from the following polynomial models:

$$y = a + b_1x,$$
$$y = a + b_1x + b_2x^2,$$
$$y = a + b_1x + b_2x^2 + b_3x^3, \text{ and}$$
$$y = a + b_1x + b_2x^2 + b_3x^3 + b_4x^4.$$

These are, respectively, linear, quadratic, cubic, and quartic polynomials for predicting hunter skill as a function of quail abundance. To determine K, add 1 (for error) to the number of parameters. The linear model, for example, has 2 parameters (a and b) so $K = 3$.

For regression modeling, Mallow's C_p is another criterion of model selection. It is calculated as

$$C_p \frac{SSR_p}{MSR_G} - (n - 2P)$$

where

SSR_K = residual sum of squares ($\sum[y_i - \hat{y}]^2$) for a model with P parameters and

MSR_G = mean square residual for the global model = $\dfrac{SSR_G}{df}$.

The degrees of freedom (df) for the global model are $n -$ (the number of parameters). For example, the global model above is the quartic polynomial, which has 6 parameters. The df for the global model are $18 - 6 = 12$. The model with the smallest C_p statistic receives support as the best of the models tested; however, there is no guarantee that it is the best. Note that $C_p = P$ for the global model.

All of the polynomials were supported in a predictive sense based on the R^2 statistic (Table 11-2). The simplest model (linear) explained 64% of the variation in hunter skill, whereas the most complex (quartic) explained 81%, so the latter model performed acceptably in an absolute sense. More complex models explain more

Table 11-2 Model selection analysis for polynomials used to predict hunter skill as a function of quail abundance in Arizona

Model	R^2	K	AIC_c	ΔAIC_c	C_p
Linear	0.64	3	281	0	10.8
Quadratic	0.75	4	297	16	5.4
Cubic	0.79	5	308	27	3.7
Quartic	0.81	6	316	35	5.0

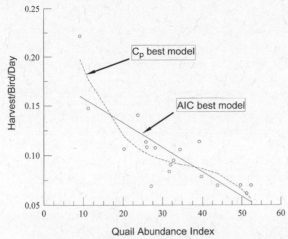

Fig. 11-1 Comparison of C_p and AIC best models for predicting hunter skill as a function of quail abundance in Arizona.

variation than less complex models, regardless of whether they are better models.

Model selection processes resulted in conflicting inference on which was the best model. The AIC_c criterion indicated the simplest model (linear) was best supported and the other models were implausible based on ΔAIC_c scores (Table 11-2). The C_p criterion, however, indicated the cubic model was better than the others, but not much better than quadratic and quartic models. The C_p criterion selected the linear model as the worst of the lot. Performance of the "best" models relative to the data appears in Fig. 11-1. This regression example, which revealed conflicting inferences from accepted model selection procedures, implies and reveals several problems with such procedures (and other statistical procedures):

* Model selection procedures are not always necessary. Indeed, any modeling might obscure simple facts. In the present example, if the purpose is simply to show the relation between hunter skill and quail abundance, then there is no need to do any statistical analysis. The scatter plot speaks for itself.

* There are many model forms (equations) that would provide a good fit to the trend. The use of polynomials was arbitrary. The point is that when researchers select model forms, they are imposing a sort of human bias on the analysis.

* More complex models might better reflect reality than simpler models. The bias-variance trade-off used as a justification for Akaike model selection is undoubtedly real in the artificial world of statistical theory, but just as undoubtedly artificial in the real world of ecological process. Do not try to impose the assumptions and protocols of statistics on nature. Keep in mind that statistics is highly artificial vis-à-vis nature.

* It so happens that independent data sets from Texas, Missouri, Oklahoma, and Kansas show a curvilinear relation between hunter skill and quail abundance that is similar to the data from Arizona. Thus, the Akaike best model, given the small set of polynomials from which it was selected, captured a fairly good but functionally imperfect image of the relationship (in a sense, it failed). This brings up another important point: always try to have an independent data set to test AIC-generated models. Any single data set should not be trusted, especially if sample size is low; therefore, Akaike best models generated from small, single data sets should not be trusted.

When to Use AIC Model Selection

The question of when to use model selection in research involves the question of why we do research. There are 3 main reasons:

1. To describe something about which we know little

2. To estimate the magnitudes of effects we know or presume exist (a form of description)

3. To test hypotheses

As we saw earlier, hypotheses address whether (does something exist?), how (what is the explanation for this event?), and why (what is the cause or underlying motivation of this event?).

Model selection has variable value, depending on why a research project is done. It might or might not be useful in description. If knowledge is so limited that models cannot be formulated, then classical descriptive work needs to take place before model selection can be applied. On the other hand, if knowledge is deep enough to advance pertinent models, then model selection might be valuable in deriving descriptive information such as an annual survival rate.

Model selection can be useful in estimating the magnitudes of effects (the strength of relationships or associations). In fact, model selection may be viewed as an algorithm to estimate magnitudes of effects. In one sense, model selection is a form of sensitivity analysis for variables in a global model because it is a method of identifying those variables that have, at most, a small effect on a response variable (Guthery, Brennan, et al. 2005).

With regard to hypothesis testing, model selection tests for the existence (whether) of patterns in the data (the global and pared models posit patterns). It is not useful for "how" questions such as, How do migratory animals navigate? It is seldom useful for "why" questions; however, it might have applications as the logistic regression example illustrated. For example, if a phenomenon causes an event, then we might deduce that a particular model will apply. If the deduced model prevails among others tested, then we have evidence in support of the hypothesized cause of an effect. However, we do not have confirmation.

In deciding when to use model selection, it is important to remember that you do not have to use it at all. You should not use model selection just because many researchers are using it. Already, we can find examples in the literature where model selection ritual has obfuscated a simple, descriptive question. Guthery, Brennan, et al. (2005:461) surmised that model selection "has become so trendy that it is being forced on research projects like Procrustes forced his victims to fit into a bed by stretching or amputating their limbs." At some times, a commonsense approach to model selection (e.g., Curtis and Jensen 2004) suffices, and this eliminates a good deal of folderol. At other times, simple description, perhaps supplemented with confidence intervals, provides full information from a study in a clear, succinct manner.

Perspectives

Natural resource research may involve selecting the best model from a collection of candidate models that predict some response (dependent variable) based on a collection of independent variables. For example, different multiple regression models might be postulated to predict some response variable. As Burnham and Anderson (2002:vii) noted, model selection may be more appropriate than statistical testing for observational studies. Indeed, it is possible to use model selection as a substitute for analysis of variance (Hilborn and Mangel 1997). The AIC is an arbitrary statistic for identifying the best (or better) models in the collection of candidate models. It is a purported method of identifying models that represent the best trade-off between bias (models too simple) and variance (models too complex). Model selection is most useful in estimating the magnitudes of known effects and testing existential hypotheses. It has limited use in description, and it is not particularly useful in addressing research hypotheses on how or why. Model selection does not eliminate the need for judgment on the part of scientists. It is perhaps best viewed as a minor but sometimes useful tool for the practitioners of natural resource science.

The introduction to model selection in this chapter contains several key points, but it is quite superficial relative to the body of knowledge about model selection. There are forms of the AIC not presented. There are many other information criteria besides the AIC (Guthery, Brennan, et al. 2005). There are techniques of model averaging that yield improved estimates of parameters and their associated variability. Burnham and Anderson (2002) provide a comprehensive treatment of the theory and practice of model selection.

However you determine the merit of a model, whether through model selection or some other process, you must recognize that statistical "significance" or "Akaike bestness" does not protect you from useless, weak, or even humorous models. You must interpret the models based on their intercepts, coefficients, and predictions to determine whether they are meritorious. Model interpretation is the topic of chapters 12 and 13.

CHAPTER 12 Interpreting Single-Variable Models

Models are metaphorical (albeit sometimes accurate) descriptions of nature, and there can never be a "correct" model.
—Ray Hilborn and Marc Mangel (1997:xii)

[W]e see 2 major errors of omission [in model selection studies]. The first is a general failure to fully interpret "best" or "plausible" models.
—Fred S. Guthery, Leonard A. Brennan, Markus J. Peterson, and Jeffrey J. Lusk (2005:461)

I've had 10 + college credits in mathematics and I still couldn't apply most of what I learned to the wildlife profession. I simply didn't learn it beyond what was required to get an A or B in the classroom. At this point I lack the aptitude to sit down with a mathematics book and make the leap from the mechanics of solving a problem to the abstract thought required to apply it to wildlife science.
—Grant Mecozzi (M.S. Candidate in Wildlife Ecology and Management, personal communication)

The last chapter concluded with the observation that "significance" or "Akaike bestness" does not preclude a model from being weak, useless, or even humorous. That circumstance provides a sort of negative motivation for model interpretation. We do not want worthless models to enter the permanent record, nor do we wish to appear doltish by publishing a worthless model. To prevent these undesirable outcomes, we must interpret models.

We have positive motivations for interpreting models, too. Models extracted from biological data contain biological information. That information is available by interpreting intercepts, coefficients, and, in some cases, the nature of a relationship between 2 variables. Sometimes models contain unexpected, hidden information that may be derived from manipulation of the model itself.

Before stating the objectives of this chapter, I offer an aside. Many natural resource scientists, younger and older, feel the same frustration over mathematics expressed by Grant Mecozzi (see epigraph). Many others look upon equations as a form of quantitative voodoo. I have been there. The first time I saw λ in a line transect density estimator, I felt as if I had lost before starting the game. So I have tried in chapters 12 and 13 to assist individuals with less developed quantitative skills by defining terms and operators and providing example calculations.

This chapter introduces the interpretation of a class of models used extensively in natural resource science. These models are selected equations where the value of a dependent variable is predicted based on the value of a single independent variable; such widely used models include linear (with or without an intercept), semi-log, and log-log. I include polynomials here because these equations simply use transformations (square, cube, . . .) of a single independent variable. The next chapter introduces interpretation of multivariable models.

Linear Models

Simple linear models (regression analysis) receive widespread use in natural resource science. They are useful when a dependent variable (y) is proportionally related to an independent variable (x).

A no-intercept linear model passes through the origin ($y = 0$ when $x = 0$). These models are of the form

$$y = bx.$$

Statistical packages provide the option of estimating the coefficient (b) for no-intercept models. The coefficient is the change in y for a 1-unit increase in x. No-intercept models are appropriate whenever y must equal 0 when x equals 0. For example: (1) In predicting absolute abundance based on an index of abundance, one assumes the index would be 0 if true abundance was 0. We will see an example of this in the next chapter. (2) In estimating the relation between age estimated from dental annuli and true age, one assumes the number of annuli would be 0 if the true age was 0.

An interesting application of the no-intercept model appeared as an early mark-recapture estimator of population size (Hayne 1949). The dependent variable was the proportion marked in the population based on a sample, and the independent variable was the number previously marked and released into the population. Recall that the regression coefficient (b) gives the increase in y for a unit increase in x. So in the mark-recapture application, b gives the increase in the proportion marked by the mark and release of 1 animal. In other words, it estimates the proportion that 1 animal represents in the population ($b = 1/N$), so by algebra $N = 1/b$.

Simple linear models with intercepts are of the form

$$y = a + bx,$$

or

$$y = a - bx,$$

where

y = the predicted value of the dependent variable,

a = the y-intercept (value of y at $x = 0$), and

b = the slope or rate of change in y as x changes.

As above, the slope may also be interpreted as the change in y for a unit increase in x. The sign $(+, -)$ of the slope indicates whether y increases $(+)$ or decreases $(-)$ with x. The sign is an important interpretive device, especially for linear equations with more than 1 independent variable (chapter 13).

The following example predicts total hunter-days (y) as a function of an abundance index (number/km; x) of bobwhites in the Rolling Plains of Texas (Guthery, Lusk, et al. 2004):

$$y = 44{,}212 + 2{,}538x.$$

The intercept (44,212) indicates the number of hunter-days if $x = 0$ (no quail). In other words, the equation predicts that 44,212 hunter-days will accumulate if there are no quail in the population. This illogical outcome illustrates the danger of extrapolating predictions beyond the range of x variables in a data set (the lowest observed x value was about 5/km). The slope (2,538) indicates that each unit increase in the population index adds 2,538 hunter-days to the total hunting effort.

The above model also contains hidden information on the relation between bobwhite abundance and harvest pressure. Indeed, the model indicates harvest pressure (hunter-days/index quail; y/x) increases at an accelerating rate as the population declines. This is evident by dividing both sides of the equation by x to obtain

$$y/x = 44{,}212/x + 2{,}538.$$

You can see that as abundance (x) becomes smaller, harvest pressure (y/x) becomes larger. For example, at $x = 20$ quail/km, harvest pressure is estimated to be 4,749 hunter-days/index quail $(y/x = 44{,}212/20 + 2{,}538 = 4{,}749)$. Reducing the population by half to 10 quail/km increases estimated harvested pressure to 6,959 hunter-days/index quail $(y/x = 44{,}212/10 + 2{,}538 = 6{,}959)$. Here is an empirical counterexample to the old saw that "harvest of quail is self-limiting." This example fits Silver's (1998:95) observation: "Sometimes when you have a set of equations and you sit down with a pencil and paper you find that they contain more than you thought they did."

Patterson and Messier (2000) estimated the following relationship between coyote (*Canis latrans*) predation of white-tailed deer (*Odocoileus virginianus*) and the abundance of snowshoe hares:

$$y = 3.0 - 0.06x$$

where

y = deer killed/coyote/100 days and

x = abundance of snowshoe hares (no./km^2).

From this equation we can estimate that (1) a coyote would kill about 3 deer in 100 days in the absence of snowshoe hares (interpretation of y-intercept with $x = 0$) and (2) each additional snowshoe hare on 1 km^2 reduces the kill of 1 coyote by 0.06 deer/100 days (interpretation of the regression coefficient). By setting y at 0 and solving for x to obtain the x-intercept, we can estimate that a density of 50 snowshoe hares/km^2 might eliminate coyote predation on deer ($0 = 3.0 - 0.06x \to x = 3.0/0.06 = 50$). That is what the model predicts, although the prediction is subject to uncertainty. If hare density exceeds 50/km^2, the kill/coyote rate (y) becomes negative, which implies that coyotes spontaneously vomit live deer. The model also indicates, in a management sense, that we could reduce coyote predation on deer by increasing the abundance of snowshoe hares or increase it by reducing hare abundance. Finally, in an ecological sense, the model shows the effects of buffer prey (hares) on the predation rate experienced by a possible target of management (white-tailed deer). Of course, whether hares or deer are a target of management is a human value.

Semi-Log Models

Semi-log models and various forms thereof also have wide application in natural resource science. The typical procedure is to take the natural logarithm of y and express it through regression analysis as a linear function of x to obtain an equation of the form

$$\ln y = a + bx.$$

This equation predicts the natural logarithm of y, which is nearly impossible to interpret. To get back to a straight prediction of y, we have to remove the logarithm, which we do by exponentiation. The operator "exp" means to raise the base of natural logarithms ($e = 2.7182$) to

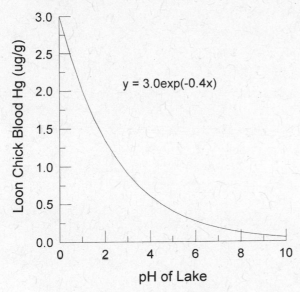

Fig. 12-1 Mercury concentration in the blood of loon chicks as a function of lake pH in Wisconsin (Merrill et al. 2005).

a power. For example, $\exp(2) = e^2 = 2.7182^2 = 7.38$. In exponentiating a semi-log model we have

$$\exp(\ln y) = \exp(a + bx)$$

from which

$$y = \exp(a + bx)$$

because $\exp(\ln y) = y$. The right side of the equation can be simplified because it is known mathematically that

$$\exp(a + bx) = \exp(a)\exp(bx).$$

Now $\exp(a)$ is just a number, or constant (k). For example, $\exp(-0.5)$ = 0.6. So, substituting,

$$y = k\exp(bx).$$

Here is an example (Merrill et al. 2005; Fig. 12-1). I exponentiated their semi-log equation,

$$\ln y = 1.09 - 0.4x,$$

to obtain

$$y = 3.0\exp(-0.4x)$$

where

y = blood mercury levels (μg/ml) in common loon chicks (*Gavia immer*) and

x = the pH of lakes in Wisconsin (observed range = 5–10).

The intercept is k; that is, if $x = 0$, $y = 3.0$ or the estimated mercury levels at a pH of 0; note that exp(0) = 1. To graphically interpret the relationship, arbitrarily create x values (e.g., 0.0, 0.5, 1.0, . . . , 10.0). Then determine predicted y values for these x values. For example, at $x = 2.0$ we have $y = 3.0\exp[-0.4(2)] = 3.0\exp(-0.8) = 1.35$.

The Merrill et al. (2005) equation can be expressed in different form to add another interpretive angle:

$$y = 3.0(0.67^x).$$

It is true that

$$e^{ab} = e^{a(b)}.$$

Thus,

$$e^{-0.4x} = e^{-0.4(x)} = 0.67^x.$$

We have discovered that each 1-unit increase in pH is associated with a 0.67, or 67%, retention of contamination levels, and this value holds through all pH levels measured, at least under the model. This is a property of the exponential decay model $[y = k\exp(-bx)]$.

We can also postulate exponential growth models of the form

$$y = k\exp(bx).$$

Note that we have gone from a negative to a positive coefficient (b).

Log-Log Models

Another widely encountered model is the log-log model, or

$$\ln y = a + b\ln x.$$

The parameters a and b may be obtained through least squares regression on the log-transformed variables. To get rid of the logarithms and obtain an equation that predicts y directly, we exponentiate both sides,

$$\exp(\ln y) = \exp(a + b\ln x)$$

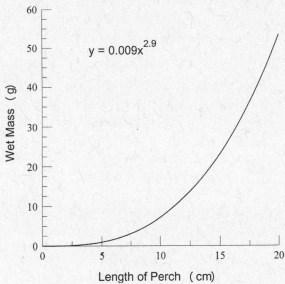

Fig. 12-2. Wet mass of perch as a function of their length (Merrill et al. 2005).

from which

$$y = kx^b.$$

Merrill et al. (2005) reported that the logarithm of wet mass (y, g) of yellow perch (*Perca flavescens*) could be modeled as a function of the logarithm of their length (x, cm; Fig. 12-2) according to

$$\ln y = -4.7 + 2.9 \ln x.$$

Upon solving for y, this equation yields

$$y = 0.009x^{2.9}.$$

Because $0^{2.9} = 0$, the intercept of this equation is 0.0. The value of the exponent of x (2.9) makes sense. We used a linear measurement (length) to predict the mass of a volume of perch (a cubic measure). In a world not variable, the value of the exponent might have been 3.0 instead of 2.9. We can say the wet mass of a perch is approximately proportional to the cube of its length. Graphing the relationship involves creating arbitrary x values and deriving predictions from these. Fig. 12-2 uses x values ranging from 0 to 20; if $x = 10$, $y = 0.009(10^{2.9})$ = 7.15.

Whenever the value of the x exponent is between 0 and 1, we

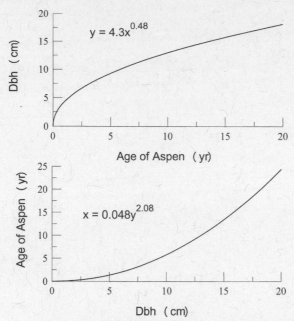

Fig. 12-3 *Top:* Diameter breast height (dbh) of aspen as a function of tree age (Rolstad et al. 2000). *Bottom:* Age of aspen as a function of dbh (determined by solving for *x* from the top graph).

have a model wherein the dependent variable increases with some root of x. For example, $x^{0.5}$ is the square root of x. Perhaps the most widely known example of this function is the species-area curve from island biogeography (Shafer 1990),

$$S = kA^z,$$

where

S = the number of species on an island,

k = a constant,

A = the size of the island (e.g., ha), and

z = some root of A between 0 and 1.

Rolstad et al. (2000) used an exponentiated log-log model to predict the stem dbh (diameter breast height, cm) of aspen (*Populus tremuloides*) based on the age (years) of a tree (Fig. 12-3):

$$y = 4.3x^{0.48}.$$

This model indicates dbh = 0 cm when age = 0. Then, dbh increases approximately in proportion to the square root of age because the exponent is 0.48.

Note that we can use the Rolstad et al. (2000) model to predict age of aspen based on dbh. This is a matter of solving the original equation for x (age). The resulting formula is

$$x = 0.048 y^{2.08}.$$

Thus, whereas dbh increased approximately in proportion to the square root of age, age increases approximately in proportion to the square of dbh.

Polynomials

Polynomials are functions of the form

$$y = a + b_1 x + b_2 x^2 + \ldots + b_k x^k$$

where b_k does not equal 0. A linear function $y = a + bx$ with $b \neq 0$ is a polynomial of degree 1 (x raised to the first power); a quadratic function $y = a + b_1 x + b_2 x^2$ with $b_i \neq 0$ is a polynomial of degree 2 (x raised to the second power); and so on. Polynomials are useful in that many types of functions, including logarithmic and exponential functions, can be approximated to any desired degree of accuracy. Indeed, a polynomial of high enough order will fit almost any data set. For example, a quadratic polynomial can provide a perfect fit to exactly 3 data points with different x values, a cubic polynomial to 4 data points, a quartic polynomial to 5 data points, and so on. This is a dangerous property of polynomials because a good fit may lead to absurd predictions, especially with small sample sizes and higher-ordered polynomials. In natural resource science polynomials higher than degree 3 are rare.

Polynomials have 2 main benefits in modeling. First, they provide a means of invoking curvature in the relation between a dependent and an independent variable. A second benefit in simple curve fitting is that any polynomial of order 2 or higher has a variety of shapes (curves) contained in the response. For example, sections of a cubic polynomial will appear to have upper asymptotes and lower asymptotes, to show exponential declines and increases, and depending on scaling, to appear linear (Fig. 12-4).

Stewart et al. (2000) used a quadratic polynomial to describe

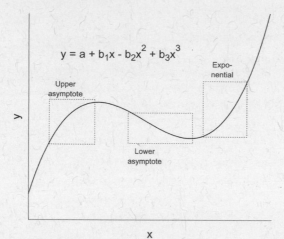

Fig. 12-4 Various curve types along a cubic polynomial model.

the relationship between white-tailed deer use of different plots as a function of an index of carrying capacity (amount of food) on plots (Fig. 12-5). Their model was

$$y = 0.01 + 0.03x - 0.003x^2$$

where

y = average number of deer/scan sample on a plot (deer use) and

x = an index to carrying capacity on a plot.

As an example, if $x = 5$, then $y = 0.01 + 0.03(5) - 0.003(5^2) = 0.085$. Interpretation of the relationship indicates practically no deer use at a carrying capacity index of 0, maximum use at an index of 5, and no use at indexes >10. The carrying capacity associated with maximum use may be estimated by examining the graph for the maximum value of the quadratic function or calculated exactly using calculus or algebra.

The model would appear to have some problems. After the carrying capacity index exceeded about 5, why would deer use decline? They would have more food. It turns out that plots with the highest carrying capacity had too much woody cover (i.e., food), which impeded deer use (Stewart et al. 2000).

Look at the low values for average number of deer/plot in the figure. Look at the nature of the quadratic relationship. Do you see that (1) in the range of carrying capacities of 2–8, carrying capacity made little difference in deer use, and (2) in the range 4–6, deer use

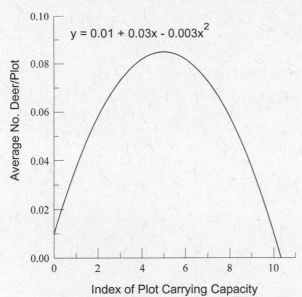

Fig. 12-5 White-tailed deer use of plots as a function of plot carrying capacity (Stewart et al. 2000).

was almost independent of carrying capacity (flat part of curve)? These are some biological and management interpretations we can draw from the Stewart et al. curve.

Perspectives

Single-variable models (equations) of the form $y = f(x)$ may be used as predicting equations or descriptions of relationships. The parameters (intercept, coefficients) in single-variable models often provide information relevant to assessing the quality of a model and drawing biological or management inferences from the model. Study of the graphs of these models may show them to be of questionable value or may reveal additional information of biological or management relevance. Graphing a relationship involves creating a set of arbitrary x values, plugging these into the predicting equation, and determining the associated y values.

I doubt if there is any simple, comprehensive algorithm to apply in model interpretation. Certainly it is a good idea to examine intercepts and coefficients to determine whether they make sense. You might have to transform models into a homologue to interpret them. For example, $\ln y = a + b\ln x$ is difficult to interpret, but $y = kx^b$ is tractable because you can directly graph how y changes with x.

·You might have to study figures of published relationships, or you might have to develop your own graphs to determine further information contained in models. Be sure to look at the range of values of the dependent variable to see whether any predicted response is meaningful.

We turn next to multivariable models. These models are more difficult to interpret to the point of being beyond human comprehension.

CHAPTER 13

Interpreting Multivariable Models

Well, that is my fate: and it is as natural for us Flatlanders to lock up a Square for preaching the Third Dimension, as it is for you Spacelanders to lock up a Cube for preaching the Fourth.
—Edwin A. Abbot (1992:viii)

It is often helpful to think of the four coordinates of an event as specifying its position in a four-dimensional space called space-time. It is impossible to imagine a four-dimensional space. I personally find it hard enough to visualize three-dimensional space!
—Stephen W. Hawking (1988:24)

Edwin A. Abbott (1838–1926) published *Flatland: A Romance in Many Dimensions* in 1884. The book was about a culture that lived in 2 dimensions. This sexist culture was highly class conscious. Women, the lowest class, were straight lines. The social scale for men ranged from lower-class isosceles triangles to middle-class squares to upper-class circles. It was heresy in Flatland to consider a third or, heaven forbid, a fourth or higher dimension.

We lived in 2 dimensions (Flatland) in chapter 12. Now we move into Spaceland (3 dimensions) and Hyperspaceland (>3 dimensions). Vexing concepts, such as infinity, will attend our immigration, and we will come to see that Hyperspaceland may be viewed only in an arbitrary and incomplete fashion.

This chapter begins with a discussion of dimensions and defines the concept of hyperspace. Then I provide examples of multivariable models from multiple and logistic regression and show how these models may be interpreted analytically and graphically.

Dimensions of Relations

With respect to models, an equation with a single dependent and independent variable has 2 dimensions. A model with a single dependent variable and 2 independent variables has 3 dimensions. If the number of independent variables exceeds 2, the dimension of the model exceeds 3.

We can graphically visualize relationships in 2 (chapter 12) or 3 dimensions on 2-dimensional paper (Fig. 13-1). Commercial software is available for plotting 3-dimensional graphs.

There are 2 other ways to visualize 3 dimensions on 2-dimensional paper. We could view a curvilinear response surface

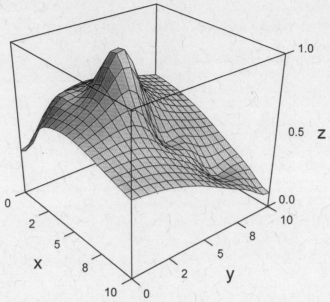

Fig. 13-1 Three-dimensional graphic in 2 dimensions and an example of a response surface.

(prediction surface for an equation; Fig 13-1 is an example) as a homologue to landscape topography and then plot contours as is done on topographic maps. The technique first involves setting a contour value (arbitrary values of the dependent variable). Then we select an arbitrary set of values for 1 independent variable and solve for the corresponding value of the other independent variable. The pairs of values for the 2 independent variables along a contour are then plotted. The contour technique would show peaks, valleys, and flatlands in the response surface just as a topographic map shows these landscape features. I have not seen this technique used in natural resource science, but it is available.

The third alternative is simpler. It involves plotting the dependent variable as a function of 1 independent variable at different fixed values of the second independent variable. We will see application of this technique in the logistic regression example that follows.

For >3 dimensions, we can graphically visualize only slices of hyperspace. By slices of hyperspace, I mean portions of the response surface that are exceedingly thin because additional independent variables are held constant. For example, given a dependent variable and 3 independent variables, we could hold one of the independent variables constant, which yields a specific number. This number is added to the intercept, and the resulting model (1 dependent, 2 independent variables) can be plotted as in Fig. 13-1. There are infinitely many slices in hyperspace, and it would take eternity to view them all. Nonetheless, we can make rational decisions on what the values of constants are; we would suppose modes or means would capture the general nature of the response to variables not held constant. However, it must be realized that our ability to reliably interpret multivariable models wanes rapidly as the number of independent variables increases, and eventually, the models are *beyond human comprehension*. Many models appearing in the ecological literature today are incomprehensible.

Multiple Linear Regression
Multiple linear regression involves ≥ 2 independent (x) variables in a model of the form

$$y = a + b_1 x_1 + b_2 x_2 + \ldots + b_k x_k,$$

where

y = the predicted value of the dependent variable,

a = the y-intercept or the value of y if all independent variables $x_i = 0$, and

b_i = the rate of change in y for a unit increase in the variable x_i if you hold all other x values constant.

If a model has the property that no independent variable is a function of the other independent variables (e.g., no interaction terms or powers of x_i), then the signs ($+$, $-$) of the coefficients (b_i) show the direction of the change in y as x_i increases, holding other x_i at fixed values. Simply by looking at the coefficients, you can do some analytical interpretation of a multiple regression model. Given the conditions specified above, does it make sense that y declines (negative coefficient) or increases (positive coefficient) with some x variable? If it does not make sense, there is something wrong with the model, the data, or your understanding of nature.

Here is an example of a multiple linear regression model from Ellis et al. (1972). Their goal was to develop equations to predict prehunt density (y; birds/40 ha) of bobwhites on 2 state parks in Illinois. Independent variables were March (prebreeding) density (x_1), the average number of "bobwhite" calls for 2-minute listening stops (x_2), and the average number of calling males/stop (x_3). Data were collected for 8 consecutive years on each of the 2 study areas. The resulting models were

$$y_1 = 15.9 - 0.4x_1 + 3.0x_2 - 10.3x_3 \text{ for study area 1,}$$

and

$$y_2 = 4.9 - 0.8x_1 + 0.6x_2 + 0.3x_3 \text{ for study area 2.}$$

How do we interpret these models?

First, area 1 would have about 16 bobwhites/40 ha and area 2 about 5 bobwhites/40 ha in the prehunt population if no birds were present in the breeding population and no calling males were heard. This conclusion is based on the intercept (first term on the right side of the equal sign). So the intercepts do not make sense and possibly represent extrapolation beyond the range of the data, which is often the case where at least some of the x_i values are >0 for all data points.

Second, if other independent variables are held constant, prehunt density declined at a rate of 0.4 birds/bird in the breeding population (x_1) on area 1 and at 0.8 birds/bird on area 2. This is based on the negative coefficients for x_1. This result makes no sense; that is, we would expect prehunt density to increase with breeding density.

Third, if other independent variables are held constant, prehunt density increased on both areas, as total calls (x_2) increased based on positive regression coefficients. This result makes sense. More calls imply more males imply higher prehunt densities.

Fourth, if other independent variables are held constant, prehunt density declined with calling males/stop (x_3) on area 1 (negative coefficient) and increased with this variable on area 2 (positive coefficient). This result is self-contradictory. Why would prehunt density be negatively related with males/stop on 1 area and positively related on the other?

Upon interpretation, the models given above appear to be quite bad even though they were statistically significant. The contradictory and counterintuitive results may have resulted from the independent variables being highly correlated, resulting in the problem of multicollinearity, a condition where ≥ 1 independent variable(s) are nearly a linear combination of the others. This condition may result in nonsensical coefficients in multiple regression analysis. With data pooled over both areas ($n = 16$), we find the correlation between x_1 and x_2 is 0.72, between x_1 and x_3 is 0.66, and between x_2 and x_3 is 0.93. The relatively high correlations among independent variables, especially x_2 and x_3, indicate that only 1 of them should be used for developing a prediction equation because in a modeling context these 2 variables are essentially the same; one provides no information not already contained in the other.

Logistic Regression

Natural resource scientists widely use logistic regression to model dependent variables that assume values between 0 and 1. Such variables might include survival or mortality rates, or the probability of a binary variable such as (absent, present), (survived, died), or (failed, succeeded). A logistic regression model is an approximate homologue of logistic population growth, except that the logistic regression model has a carrying capacity (K in population modeling) of 1. Simple (1 independent variable) logistic regression models have the typical S-shaped curve as the graph of the proportion or probability being modeled, the shape of which (forward, reverse) depends on the sign ($+$, $-$) of the coefficient of the independent variable (Fig. 13-2).

The data for this example came from Curtis and Jensen (2004). They used logistic regression modeling to predict the presence (1) or absence (0) of beavers (*Castor canadensis*) at culverts and bridges in New York. The independent variables appearing in 1 logistic model were

$x_1 =$ stream gradient (%),

$x_2 =$ area without woody plant canopy (%),

$x_3 =$ stream width (m), and

$x_4 = x_1 x_2 =$ the interaction of stream gradient and open area (% $-$ %).

With these variables the model has 4 instead of 5 dimensions because of the interaction term ($x_4 = x_1 x_2$ does not add a dimension).

Computer-assisted logistic regression analysis yields the log-transformed (logit) version of the logistic model:

$$\text{logit } P(X)$$
$$= \ln\{P(X)/[1 - P(X)]\} = a + b_1 x_1 + b_2 x_2 + b_3 x_3 + b_4 x_4$$

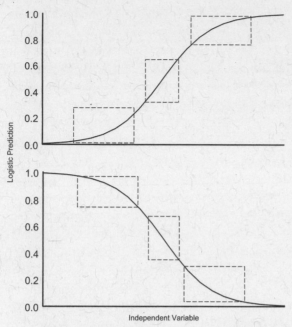

Fig. 13-2 Forward (*top*) and reverse (*bottom*) logistic curves. The dashed boxes contain various manifestations of logistic curves that might appear within the range of data values used in logistic regression modeling.

where by exponentiating

$$P(X) = 1/(1 + \exp\{-[\text{logit } P(X)]\}).$$

This looks intimidating, but interpretation is fairly simple. The term $P(\boldsymbol{X})$ simply represents the logistic function with a carrying capacity of 1, and the boldface $\boldsymbol{X}$ indicates the list of parameters in the model (a, b_1, b_2, b_3, b_4). Notice the negative $(-)$ sign preceding the argument (numbers to be exponentiated) of the exponentiation operator in the expression for $P(\boldsymbol{X})$. The presence of this negative sign changes the sign of the intercept and all coefficients that follow in the expression for logit $P(\boldsymbol{X})$.

Curtis and Jensen (2004) reported the logistic regression model

$$\text{logit } P(X) = 7.423 - 1.627x_1 - 0.094x_2 - 0.330x_3 + 0.016x_4.$$

The logistic function derived from this model is

$$P(X) =$$
$$1/[1 + \exp(-7.423 + 1.627x_1 + 0.094\,x_2 + 0.330x_3 - 0.016x_4)].$$

Notice that signs changed for the intercept and coefficients in the logit model when we converted it to the logistic prediction model. If you plug in values for the *x* variables in the $P(X)$ function, you obtain a number between 0 and 1. You can view this number as an estimate of the probability of beaver presence, given the values of the independent variables used to calculate it.

As in multiple linear regression, it might be informative to estimate the prediction if all $x_i = 0$ (substitute 0 for all x_i in the equation). For the Curtis and Jensen model, we obtain

$$P(X) = 1/\{1 + \exp[-7.423 + 1.627(0) + 0.094(0) + 0.330(0)$$
$$- 0.016(0)]\} = 1/[1 + \exp(-7.423)] = 0.99.$$

We have predicted presence of beavers on a placid stream (no gradient) with much food (0% open) that has no water (stream width = 0 m). This may be our familiar problem of extrapolating beyond the range of the data used to construct a model because a data point where all independent variables were 0 probably did not occur. If you use model selection to identify best logistic regression models, and if the routine selects the intercept-only model (which happens), you are predicting a constant. This implies the prediction is independent of other variables tested as predictors. It further implies your model is very probably pathetic, even if it is Akaike best.

Also as in multiple linear regression, the sign $(-, +)$ of logit coefficients are directly interpretable if the model contains no independent variable that is a function of other independent variables, for example, interaction terms. If other variables are held constant, a negative logit coefficient indicates that $P(X)$ declines curvilinearly as x_i increases, and a positive logit coefficient indicates that $P(X)$ increases curvilinearly as x_i increases. You can use these facts to judge whether a logistic regression model makes sense. One has to be careful, however, in interpreting the sign of a logit coefficient because we are in a nonlinear realm that has flat parts, and the logistic equation itself provides a potpourri of curves (Fig. 13-2).

The Curtis and Jensen (2004) model is slightly more difficult to interpret because of the interaction term ($x_4 = x_1 x_2$). One way to interpret the implication of a variable contained in an interaction is to determine the sign of the effective coefficient at the mean value of the other variable in the interaction. Holding percent open constant at its mean (~33%), we obtain

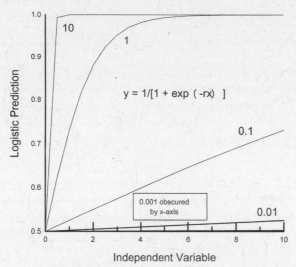

Fig. 13-3 Effects of the magnitude of logistic regression coefficients on logistic curves.

$$b_1 + 33(b_4) = -1.627 + 33(0.016) = -1.099$$

as the coefficient for stream gradient. The negative value implies that the probability of beaver presence declines as gradient increases if percent open is held constant at its mean. To interpret the implication of percent open area if gradient is held constant at its mean (~1.3%), we have

$$b_2 + 1.3(b_4) = -0.094 + 1.3(0.016) = -0.073$$

as the coefficient for percent open area. If gradient is held constant at its mean, the probability of beaver presence declines as percent open area increases. Under average conditions, we would expect beavers to disappear as gradient increases and food becomes less plentiful. The negative value for stream width is difficult to interpret, as is the positive value for the interaction coefficient. As a point of interest, the model predicts a low probability (0.003) of presence of beavers in waterfalls with no food (100% gradient, 100% open).

A final diagnostic in interpreting logistic regression models is the magnitude of a coefficient (Fig. 13-3). Coefficients near 0 (e.g., −0.003, 0.005) might imply the x variable associated with the coefficient has little or no predictive value. The reason is that such coefficients might, for all intents and purposes, predict a number that is nearly constant [$\exp(-0.003) = 0.997$, $\exp(0) = 1$, $\exp(0.005) =$

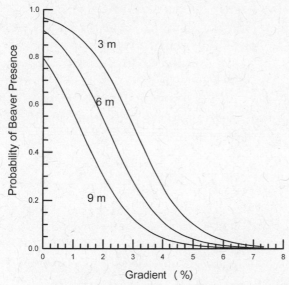

Fig. 13-4 Logistic regression predictions of the probability of beaver presence at bridges and culverts in New York as a function of stream gradient and stream width (Curtis and Jensen 2004).

1.005]. Indeed, logistic regression coefficients near 0 might indicate an essentially null response, despite whether they are significant or a member of the Akaike best family of parameters. On the other hand, coefficients near 0 can be quite meaningful, depending on the units of measure for both the independent and dependent variables.

Let us graphically examine the predictions associated with stream gradient at different stream widths (3, 6, 9 m) with percent open area held constant at its mean (~33%; Fig. 13-4). The relationship would change for different stream widths or if open area was held constant at a different value (the problem of hyperspace). For the interaction term, I used $33x_1$ (mean percent open area × gradient). So in interpreting this figure, we should qualify with "under average conditions for percent open area." We created arbitrary values for gradient (0%, 0.5%, 1.0%, . . . , 8.0%) to model on with stream width held at a specified value. For example, for a gradient of 1.0% and a stream width of 3 m,

$$P(X) = 1/\{1 + \exp[-7.423 + 1.627(1) + 0.094(33) + 0.330(3) - 0.016(1)(33)]\} = 0.9.$$

Under the conditions given, Fig. 13-4 indicates that the probability of beaver presence declined with gradient at all values of stream width examined. This result is the same as obtained by interpreting the logit coefficient, but the graphic provides information on the shape of the relationship. Likewise, at any fixed gradient, except in the right tails of the curves, the probability of beaver presence declined as stream width increased. This can be interpreted to indicate that beavers were less sensitive to gradient in narrower streams (or more sensitive to gradient in broader streams). To reiterate, Fig. 13-4 shows a method of examining a 3-dimensional problem in 2 dimensions.

Perspectives

Multivariable models are amenable to interpretation in the same sense as single-variable models, but they obviously are more complex. These models may be interpreted analytically and graphically. Analytically, one should first check the intercept to determine whether it represents a logical or illogical outcome. Whether the coefficients are positive or negative in multiple regression models can be interpreted as to whether the dependent variable should trend in a negative or positive direction. Does the sign of a coefficient make biological sense? You have to decide.

Contrariwise, a negative coefficient in logistic regression indicates higher predictions as an *x* variable increases, whereas a positive coefficient indicates the opposite. Do these trends make biological sense? Again, you have to decide. Be sure to critically examine coefficients near 0 in logistic regression analysis because they might indicate a useless variable in the model.

Graphical interpretation of multivariable models is fairly straightforward in 3 dimensions (1 dependent, 2 independent variables) and amenable to plotting on 2-dimensional paper. For models with >3 dimensions, you have to arbitrarily hold nonplotted independent variables constant at rational values such as modes or means. Upon doing this, you are drawing slices from hyperspace and interpreting those slices, of which there are infinitely many. Be careful.

The main point of this chapter is that you would be wise to interpret the multivariable models you develop at a deeper level than "statistical significance" or "Akaike bestness," especially when you are modeling in hyperspace. Interpretation means evaluating the model analytically and, in a sense, modeling with the model (graphics) to see what it implies. Interpretation will provide additional information from a model, and it might prevent the publication of embarrassing models.

Up to this point in the book, we have discussed the nature of science and the nature of the quantitative tools in the scientist's toolkit. These quantitative tools have an insidious property: they tend to take over the minds of scientists and cause them to misperceive the relative importance of means and ends. I address this problem in chapter 14.

CHAPTER 14 **Means, Ends, and** *Shoulds*

> *Suppose . . . that we require a house to protect us from inclement weather and*
> *that a hammer is needed for construction. The tendency of modern society*
> *eventually would be to focus on perfecting the hammer, rather than building the*
> *house—thus transmuting means into ends.*
> —Fred S. Guthery, Jeffrey J. Lusk, and Markus J. Peterson (2001:383)

> *It is not necessary in any empirical science to keep an elaborate*
> *logicomathematical system always apparent, any more than it is necessary*
> *to keep a vacuum cleaner conspicuously in the middle of a room at all times.*
> *When a lot of irrelevant litter has accumulated, the machine must be brought*
> *out, used, and then put away.*
> —G. Evelyn Hutchinson (1957:415)

> *The practice of natural resource science has become a game of methodological*
> *"Gotcha!" rather than a search for insightful and reliable knowledge about*
> *natural resources.*
> —Steven W. Buskirk (University of Wyoming, personal communication)

Are scientific methods (means) more important than knowledge (end), or is knowledge more important than scientific methods? Most scientists would agree that knowledge is the more important of the two, but they would condition that opinion on the fact that sound methods are essential for growing knowledge. From my perspective, however, a major problem in natural resource science is an operational reversal in the importance of means and ends.

When the culture of science transmutes means and ends, a series of unfortunate mind-sets ensues. These mind-sets stifle thought and imagination, engender reaction rather than reason, and create contradictions regarding what is and what should be in natural resource science. Worst of all, the mind-sets divert or inhibit ideas on the nature of nature and thereby inhibit progress in knowing and understanding.

This chapter expands on the ideas mentioned above. I start by enumerating problems that arise from the transmutation of means and ends. The auxiliary verb *should* frequently inhabits descriptions of methodology. This pairing leads to contradiction between what is and what should be in natural resource science, which I address. In the final section I dissect the auxiliary verb *should* as it relates to the conduct of natural resource science and find that most *shoulds* are narrowly focused, whereas a rare few cut across the entire scientific enterprise.

Means versus Ends

The epigraph by Guthery, Lusk, et al. (2001) illustrates a human tendency that plays out in natural resource science as reverence for quantitative methods (e.g., statistical tests, model selection), which are means. Practitioners become progressively more and more enamored of the methods and progressively less and less concerned about the knowledge derived by applying the methods. Means supplant the search for knowledge as the most important factor in research. Papers become judged on their adherence to accepted methodology, rather than on their potential contribution to our understanding of nature. The finding of a significant difference or best model becomes the goal of research; ecological interpretation of a difference or best model seemingly becomes irrelevant. *Shoulds* (mandated behaviors) associated with quantitative methods become etched in the minds of scientists, and reaction thereby replaces reasoning as a mode of interpretation and judgment. Science becomes ritualistic, formulaic, and unimaginative.

Now I am most certainly not suggesting that natural resource scientists limit or abandon quantitative methods; most practicing scientists strongly *believe* that quantitative methodology is the sine qua non of sound science. (I think the belief is misplaced because I believe ideas are the essential condition of science.) I am suggesting, however, that we keep quantitative methods in better perspective relative to the end we desire—knowledge. Subservience to quantitative methodology leads to nonsense such as naked P-values, meaningless significant differences that are not recognized as meaningless, and worthless Akaike best models that are not recognized as worthless. These events manifest because the spawn of methodology, not knowledge, comes to be identified as the accomplishment.

When methodological *shoulds* insinuate themselves upon the minds of scientists, science takes on a sort of spiritual posture. The word *should* implies a background condition or value. "If this condition or value prevails, then you should . . ." Really, under a condition or value, we have, "If this condition or value prevails, then you *must* . . ." So *should* and *must* may be taken as synonyms meaning "to be compelled to in order to satisfy some condition that exists and is agreed upon (value)." If you want to obtain an unbiased estimate of a population mean, then you must randomly sample the population. If you want to use classical statistical inference as a method of gathering knowledge, then you must apply classical experimental design. Notice that use of classical statistical inference (i.e., analysis of variance) is the condition that mandates classical experimental design. With respect to the conduct of natural resource science the words *should* or *must* usually apply conditionally, not generally.

This lack of generality is important to keep in mind, for it implies that no single methodological approach to the conduct of science prevails over all others. Unfortunately, the word *should* takes thinking from the conditional to the mandatory. The conditions outside of which a *should* prevails are not and perhaps cannot be part of thought processes. The imagination is therefore limited to the mode of research consistent with the *should*. This occurs because thoughts on methodology saturate space-time in the mind and leave little room for thoughts on how nature operates. Some of the *shoulds* also put bounds on thought possibilities. A good example is Garton et al.'s (2005) assertion that research *should be* experimental. If that *should be* prevailed across all of natural resource science, then the thickness of our journals would diminish substantially and progress in knowledge accumulation would be slowed because observational studies would no longer be published.

The *shoulds* of science are akin to the values of cultures, and, therefore, most presumed *shoulds* are arguable. Consider: you *should* have an experimental control. If so, then you *should not* do a case study because there is no experimental control. And yet case studies may be informative and lead to improved understanding and management. Where would history, archaeology, and paleontology be without case studies?

I caution students of natural resource science that some, perhaps most, practicing scientists will view my questioning of experimental design as heretical if not idiotic. The belief in experimental design is so firmly entrenched as to be an article of faith and, therefore, a part of the religion of science. I counter with the observation that experimental design forces one to use the null hypothesis. I view the null as nonscientific because it is mindless and, in general, a priori false (chapter 10). I also counter with the observation that among many classic works in natural resource science, *Game Management* (Leopold 1933), *The Natural Regulation of Animal Numbers* (Lack 1954), and *On the Origin of Species* (Darwin 1859) relied on neither *P*-values, Akaike best models, nor experimental design.

Philosophical Quagmires

The alert student who has read articles on the philosophy of natural resource science will come to realize that the *shoulds* of our science have landed us in a philosophical quagmire. On the one hand, we extol deduction (Romesburg 1981) and question induction as a basis of knowledge. "Research *should be* designed to test [deductions from research] hypotheses" (Garton et al. 2005:46; emphasis added). On the other hand, we are perfectly satisfied to induce from a sample to a population (statistical tests). We apply model selection with some abandon, and this tool is strictly inductive in the vast majority of applications. We generalize (induce) without second thought in the "Management Implications" sections of our journals. There is a major disconnect, in short, between what we claim our science should be (experimental, H-D) and what it is (largely observational).

The disconnect between what *should be* and what *is* manifests in various ways, none useful. The gratuitous predictions (in the guise of deductions) that appear in objectives statements are an example. Only authors know the contents of their minds when they make gratuitous predictions. Some may be merely aping what appears to be trendy and tribally sanctioned wording. Others might believe that by making predictions, they are automatically doing H-D science; this is not so unless a research hypothesis entailed the prediction. To me it seems these authors are innocently building facades that unnecessarily and even clumsily detract from the information contained in a manuscript. It is all a tad bit disingenuous.

In fairness, though, we have a situation where authors may be acting without understanding. They believe what they are doing is correct; the belief must be founded, to some degree, in ignorance of the nature of research hypotheses, deduction, and application of the H-D method. It is also founded in tribal sanction. Perhaps this book will enhance understanding.

Does it matter that natural resource science is in a philosophical quagmire? It matters at least to the extent that the pretension associated with what *should be* detracts from message by adding clutter to simple papers. Nowadays, the studies published in natural resource journals usually are either observational or, if experimental, measurements of the magnitudes of known effects. It seems to me that efficient transmission of information from author to reader is best served by eliminating verbal kitsch (e.g., gratuitous predictions) to the maximum extent possible.

Natural resource science would become more ingenuous if its practitioners would recognize and promote what they do frequently and well. These accomplishments fall into 4 general categories. First, by dint of training, experience, and inclination, natural resource scientists tend to be skilled natural historians (plants and animals). Their efforts range from the measurement of simple life history traits to analysis of structural and successional affiliations of species and communities. Radiotelemetry studies, widely reported in ecological journals, are basically natural history projects to obtain information on survival, cover selection and use, movements, and ranges. Natural history studies are crucial contributors to our knowledge base.

Second, natural resource scientists have a traditional bent to develop and evaluate methods and techniques. Such efforts frequent the pages of our journals and have done so for decades. For example, the second edition of the wildlife techniques manual (Mosby 1963) was 419 pages, whereas the sixth edition (Braun 2005) was 974 pages. Methods and techniques development leads to improved measurement, and this, in turn, leads to improved reliability of the knowledge gained from measurement.

Third, natural resource scientists devote considerable effort to estimating the shape and strength of relations in nature. "The aim of science," wrote Poincaré (1952:xxiv), "is not things themselves . . . , but the relations between things; outside those relations there is no reality knowable." An important part of observational science is assessing the nature of relations, and natural resource scientists are skilled at assessing relations. Information-theoretic model selection is the tool du jour for such assessments. These assessments help in understanding patterns and processes, and they serve as a basis for management decisions.

Fourth, we also devote considerable effort to estimating magnitudes of known or presumed effects. At this time, natural resource science generally lacks original hypotheses to test in the field. A good deal of our research is therefore directed at retracing old studies in new times and places under known relationships. This is perhaps a general property of research nowadays (Edwards 1992:2). "Most studies today are local demonstrations of things we already know," observes a colleague, Samuel D. Fuhlendorf of Oklahoma State University. Such studies may appear in the guise of experimental science and may be accompanied by mundane hypotheses, but in fact they are descriptive studies of the magnitudes of known effects. There is merit in estimating the magnitudes of known effects, and the community of natural resource scientists is accomplished at doing so, given the variability with which we must deal. At a minimum, magnitude-of-effect studies provide inductive knowledge and fodder for discerning patterns and relationships.

If I have correctly identified what we do well and frequently, then our forte is observational science. Accordingly, field-oriented scientists perhaps might accept description as an often inevitable and entirely appropriate condition of their research. We operate in an uncontrollable, multivariate, curvilinear world with feedback and interference; our research world is analogous to that of sociologists, economists, and epidemiologists, among others. A reasonable goal for improving our science, therefore, might be extraction from these systems of fundamental, reliable descriptive facts (inductions) upon which to build theory and practice. The reliability of the knowledge we build then depends to some extent upon the reliability of our inductive knowledge foundation.

Facts from descriptive natural history could serve as the foundation for natural resource science. With facts of natural history there are no questions of how or why because the answer to the former is evolution and to the latter is adaptation. Accordingly, I view natural history as the arithmetic of natural resource science because it consists of the purest facts with which we deal; facts of natural history are, in an ecological sense, tantamount to the axioms of mathematicians and the molecules of chemists. Natural history provides a trustworthy point of divergence for establishing principles, developing hypotheses on processes and patterns in nature, and judging the reliability of inductions. Comprehensive knowledge of natural history might lead to pinnacles of science with the discovery of simple rules that reveal order in apparent chaos, such as Darwin's theory of natural selection.

The mention of Darwin's theory reminds me that one of my goals in writing this book was to revive, vitalize, and in some cases vivify the elegant aspects of natural resource science not associated with quantitative methods, experimental design, and their external parasites (the *shoulds*). That revivification entails relegating quantitative methods to a secondary role in the grander pursuits of science, which are ideas.

Let me mention several ideas that vitalize natural resource science: The principle of inversity (density-dependent production).

Additive versus compensatory harvest mortality; the threshold of security. The principle of edge. Carrying capacity. Fragmentation and
metapopulations. Population viability. Niche gestalt. Usable space.
Slack in the configuration of habitat patches. Buffer prey. The search
image. Scale-dependent habitat selection. Competition. Complexity.
Chaos. Foraging theory. Plant and animal succession. The handicap
principle. The theory of natural selection. It matters not that some
of these ideas have been found wanting, for that is the general fate
of ideas in science. It matters greatly that the ideas were put forward
as targets for challenge and stepping stones in the accrual of knowledge. Great ideas are why we extol Aldo Leopold, David Lack, Paul
Errington, Herbert Stoddard, Edward Wilson, and Charles Darwin,
among others, and forget the first name of Mr. Akaike. "[T]he measure of [natural resource] scientists is not their facility with statistical
algorithms, but rather their contributions to knowledge, understanding, and innovation in the realm of ecology" (Guthery, Brennan,
et al. 2005:463).

Reflections on *Should*

The word *should* has appeared repeatedly in this chapter. I have an
automatic aversion to the word when it purportedly applies to the
conduct of science or the behavior of scientists. Science is a sprawling
endeavor (chapter 1) not easily covered by simple mandates.

Certain of the extant *shoulds* are easily dismissed as general
mandates for scientists and are therefore matters of taste. I gave an
example earlier: "You should do experimental science under the H-D
method." Humankind has accumulated a good deal of knowledge
that ranges from useful to profound outside this *should*. The general
theory of relativity is an example. So science has certain *shoulds* that
may apply under special circumstances. Does it have any *shoulds* that
apply generally?

I think it rational to posit some general *shoulds* if the culture of
scientists can come to consensus on the human value(s) that moti-
vates the doing of science; remember that values undergird *shoulds*.
We do science to grow knowledge and to understand nature. "The
injunction to want knowledge," observes Adler (1981:79), ". . . is a
true prescription—the true statement of an ought—because human
beings all need knowledge. As Aristotle pointed out, man by nature
desires to know."

If we are by nature a species that values knowledge, then it seems to me this value entails a set of *shoulds* much like a research hypothesis entails a deduction. The entailed *shoulds* will have a common property, namely, that under their influence the practice of science is more likely to give rise to knowledge than to something else (e.g., superstition, unsupported belief, misperception). Herewith is a set of *shoulds* that I believe to be consistent with the human value and the common property.

Scientists should be scrupulously honest (chapter 1). The reason is obvious: we do not want half-truths or nontruths entering what we presume to be our repository of knowledge because we build on that repository. If science is working properly, dishonesty will be revealed, but the revelation might take a long time and the dishonesty might create false and fruitless trails. Scrupulous honesty might be as painless as being fully candid in writing methods and results. On the other hand, it might be quite painful. I have a colleague who was a few years into a study on predator ecology when he discovered that landowners on his study area were illegally distributing toxins to kill bird and mammal predators. As a scientist, he had but one option—to figuratively burn the data and end the project. This was painful because of the investment of money and time, but it was scrupulously honest.

Scientists should be skeptical of that which passes for knowledge. I earlier discussed the nature of scientific facts (chapter 4) and concluded most are wanting as purveyors of unconditional truth. I pointed out the propensity of human beings to suspend the rational for the tribal, to perceive nature according to a consensus of fellows, even if the perceptions are demonstrably wrong (chapter 5). We can add honest mistakes to the problems with facts and human nature. The upshot is that what we hold as knowledge is awash with matter that is not knowledge after all. Skepticism helps to reveal the not-knowledge that debauches our understanding of nature.

Scientists should publish their research results. If we are to grow knowledge and understand nature, we must have a permanent record of research findings.

Perspectives

In judging the material in this chapter relative to the enterprise of science, I believe three ideas are worth highlighting. First, misperceiving the relative contribution of means and ends inhibits progress in science for several reasons. Second, ecological scientists will not be remembered for their proficiency in quantitative methods, nor will that proficiency necessarily contribute to advances in knowledge and understanding. Rather, scientists will be remembered and make substantive contributions according to the original ideas they put forth to the community of scientists. Third, it would probably be wise for all scientists, young and old, to be sensitive to the so-called *shoulds* of science. Some of the *shoulds* are matters of taste and have no place in science. Some of them are narrowly focused and suppress thought and creativity. The *shoulds* that seem to encompass all of science are few. Appearance of the word *should* might well be automatically associated with the question, What is the human value behind this mandate?

One of the transcendental *shoulds* in natural resource science is the mandate to publish your research results. I expand on the topic in the next chapter.

CHAPTER 15 Publishing

Most . . . professors are very good at helping their graduate students see their thesis work into publication. There are, unfortunately, some exceptions to this general rule. Although not commonplace, we [The Journal of Wildlife Management] *do receive manuscripts that are largely unedited versions of a thesis.*
—Michael L. Morrison (2005:1313)

The scientific paper presents an immaculate appearance which reproduces little or nothing of the intuitive leaps, false starts, mistakes, loose ends, and happy accidents that actually cluttered up the inquiry.
—Robert Merton (cited in Peters and Waterman 1982:48)

Although scientists typically insist that their research is very exciting and adventurous when they talk to laymen and prospective students, the allure of this enthusiasm is too often lost in the predictable, stilted structure and language of their scientific publications.
—Kaj Sand-Jensen (2007:723)

Why publish your thesis or dissertation research? I think the reasons might be classified as egotistical, practical, and noble.

Egotistically, the publication of your work is a source of pride. This is not at all important to the world, but it is important to your world. It simply feels good to be published, in the same sense it feels good to succeed at any chancy or competitive endeavor.

On the practical side, preparation and submission of manuscripts show you have character, and publications strengthen your vita. If you submit a manuscript to a technical journal, you have shown initiative. You have taken a step that separates you from many if not most of your peers, whose findings vanish except as fusty volumes in library stacks. You have recognized and resolved debts to the entity that funded your work, the university that housed it, and the major professor who mentored it; you have shown integrity. You have had the courage to bare your person to a merciless (if metaphorical) rib kicking from referees and editors. You have, in sum, shown that you aspire to be a professional of high standard. These outcomes might tip the balance in your favor in competition for continued graduate study or permanent jobs. If the job is a career in science, publications are crucial.

I think publishing has a noble aspect, too. A published article is a contribution to all the knowledge that humankind has accumulated or will ever accumulate. That knowledge is the source of progress in understanding and explaining nature. That is what science is all about; science would collapse without a more or less permanent record of research findings.

It is one thing for me to extol the act of publishing, quite another for you to consummate it. Peer review and publishing are harsh processes, as they should be, because it is counterproductive to knowingly let error or nonsense adulterate the permanent record (error and nonsense unknowingly slip in, as we have seen). The obligation of referees and editors is to try to keep the permanent record minimally tainted with error and farce. As a result, mainstream journals typically reject 60%–70% of submissions.

The purpose of this chapter is to give you some general guidelines on actions you can take to increase the probability of getting a manuscript accepted, *given that you have data worth publishing*. The actions begin with selecting a journal and preparing a manuscript. Manuscript preparation involves issues of writing and style. If you are skilled or lucky, you will have the opportunity to revise the paper, and I offer some guidelines here. If you are unskilled or unlucky (e.g., draw harsh referees), you will suffer rejection, but that does not mean a manuscript is dead. There are different ways of dealing with a rejection. Did you notice that I used the words *lucky* and *unlucky* in addressing acceptance and rejection? Those words hardly seem appropriate for the purportedly dignified and objective process of peer review and editing, yet there is luck involved in publishing.

Selecting a Journal

The rote recommendation here is to select the leading journal in your field. For example, if you do a thesis in range science, *Rangeland Ecology & Management* might be your choice. If your work is sufficiently meritorious for a leading journal, it is to your benefit to publish there. Articles in leading journals receive wider distribution and more frequent citations than articles in other journals. On the downside, a leading journal might have high rejection rates.

Although it is not supposed to happen in science, technical journals have slants (biased perspectives) just like popular outlets. *Time,* for example, is slanted toward Republican philosophy, *Newsweek* toward Democratic philosophy. The point is that depending upon the nature of your results, you might want to submit to a leading journal that is slanted toward the results you obtained. You would not send a manuscript on the merits of spotted knapweed (*Centaurea biebersteinii*), a notorious alien plant, to *Conservation Biology*. In my dissertation work I found that coyotes killed Angora goats, especially kids, with some abandon. I suspected that these findings would be more palatable to range managers than to wildlife managers, so I submitted to the *Journal of Range Management* instead of *The Journal of Wildlife Management*. The paper was selected with little fuss at *Range Management*. Of course, I do not know how it would have been received at *Wildlife Management*.

If you and your collaborators decide that your data might not pass muster at a leading journal, then regional journals become a consideration. There are some excellent regional journals, such as the *Southwestern Naturalist, American Midland Naturalist, Prairie Naturalist,* and *Proceedings of the Southeastern Association of Fish and Wildlife Agencies*. These journals are rigorously reviewed and, in this sense, in no way inferior to what we call leading journals. Regional journals are more likely to accept papers with regional as opposed to more general interest. Such journals have the disadvantage of more limited distribution.

It is a good idea to have a prioritized list of journals in mind so that you know where you want to submit if your paper is rejected at your first choice, second choice, and so on. (You might want to give up if a paper is rejected 3 times, or resubmit after you have become famous.) Revision of a rejected manuscript for another journal may be a time-consuming process. You might have to change the slant of the paper. This is a matter of bringing to the fore issues of interest to the new outlet. For example, if you are rejected at a management journal and decide to submit to a more basic journal, you would want to highlight basic information and give less weight to management in your revision. You will have to recast the paper, and this involves many of the same activities you went through in preparing the original manuscript.

Preparing a Manuscript
Organization

The basic format of technical journals is pretty much boilerplate and contains the following topics.

1. The **Introduction,** which might or might not have a heading with that title, depending on the style (see below) of the

journal. The introduction logically takes the reader to the objectives of or hypotheses tested in the study. Typically, these topics appear in the last paragraph of the introduction.

2. Description of the **Study Area,** which places the study in an ecological context. This section assists the reader in interpreting the environment under which your results arose. It typically includes information on plant and animal communities, soils and topography, and climate.

3. Description of **Methods.** This includes detail on field and laboratory methods and statistical analyses.

4. Presentation of **Results.** Keep the information in this section strictly about results; don't interpret, speculate, or explain in results.

5. Interpretation, speculation, and explanation of your results relative to those of other researchers occur in **Discussion.** One purpose of discussion is to compare and contrast your (usually) inductive findings with the inductive findings of other authors. You might also want to discuss caveats about your work.

6. Some journals have a **Management Implications** section. The idea is to filter out informational bullets from your study that could be used in making decisions about management. I think this is an ill-advised section that is often packed with eco-clichés: "Based on our study of the constituents of rat urine, we recommend that managers increase habitat diversity." Nevertheless, the presence of this section is style at some journals.

7. Journals have an **Acknowledgments** section for authors to thank reviewers and helpers and acknowledge the source of financial support.

8. The last section is **Literature Cited,** although the actual title of the section is specific to the style of a journal.

Within the crude organizational framework just discussed, there are finer-grained issues of organization. A reader expects and deserves a logical flow of information within and between sections of a manuscript. In popular writing, that logical flow is based largely on construction or organization of the manuscript. One topic trends smoothly into the next. In technical writing, we have different levels of headings (major, minor, side) that serve as transitions between topics. I recommend that you use headings liberally within a manuscript to foster comprehensibility.

Beyond the use of headings to signify transition between topics, organization is a matter of thought. The old-fashioned outline is your ally in thinking through a manuscript. I have found that Microsoft PowerPoint® also is useful for organizing. You can make slides for topics and view them in the slide-sorter mode, where you can shuffle and edit as appropriate.

Style

The concept of style is mysterious to graduate students. A synonym for style is "publishing conventions." Almost all outlets, whether popular or technical, have style conventions that involve matters such as when to use numerals, how to use commas, what to abbreviate and how, how to construct literature citations and what to call them, how to make citations in text, typography, how to do titles and headings, and related matters. I suppose these students might assume they know style by virtue of high school and undergraduate training in grammar. I also suppose they might see issues of style as trivial and irrelevant. Nevertheless, application of the proper style is a matter of professionalism, and it is a factor in manuscript acceptance.

Here are some examples of different styles for acknowledgments. In the *Wildlife Society Bulletin* (now defunct) these appear in the last paragraph of the paper with the heading *"Acknowledgments."* indented in paragraph form (note italics, capitalization of first letter). In *The Journal of Wildlife Management* they appear as the last section in the paper with the first-level heading "**ACKNOWLEDGMENTS**" flush left (note all caps, boldface). In *Rangeland Ecology & Management* they appear as the last section in the paper with the first-level heading "**ACKNOWLEDGMENTS**" centered in the column.

These style matters seem picayune to novices as well as seasoned authors, but, nonetheless, they exist. Strict adherence to the style of the journal to which you are submitting increases the odds your paper will be accepted. When I edited the *Wildlife Society Bulletin* and *The Journal of Wildlife Management,* I automatically rejected, without benefit of review, submissions that were seriously out of style. Lapses in style indicated (1) I was dealing with a rank amateur or (2) the paper had already been rejected at another outlet, where it might have been in the proper style. Under the second hypothesis,

I would seem to have been dealing with a lazy, rank amateur. Referees also are sensitive to style, and this is a criterion upon which they judge the overall merit of a paper.

Style manuals for technical journals usually are available online. If you run across a question of style that is not addressed in the manual, try to find an example in a recent number of the journal to which you are submitting. It is not wise to look for examples in older numbers because details of style change frequently in journals.

Writing

Good data usually will be rejected on the basis of bad writing. Bad writing has several defining properties: improper grammar, wordiness, redundancy, poor organization, and incomprehensibility. Note that these properties are matters of language conventions and your personal mental abilities (e.g., organization).

Your goal as a writer is to transmit to your readers a given quantity of the purest possible information in as few words as possible. Brevity tends to increase the communication power of prose. Obviously, you can carry this too far, and at some point brevity cripples communication because it omits key information. If you are not sure whether a shorter version of your message will be received as you intended it to be, sacrifice brevity for clarity to foster comprehensibility. The referees and editors will comment on brevity as they deem appropriate.

In the interest of brevity and clarity, pundits of all stripes recommend that you write in the active voice (which I will explain below). The active voice is natural; we converse with each other in that voice. Often, but not always, the active voice is more concise than the passive voice.

Use of the active voice implies use of a transitive verb (one where the subject of the sentence acts on the object). "Dogs eat food." The subject, dogs, acts on (eats) the object, food. If we convert this to the passive voice, we obtain "Food is eaten by dogs." The subject, food, here receives action from the object, dogs. You can see that the active voice is shorter and more graceful than the passive voice in this example.

Notice that the personal pronouns *I* and *we* have nothing to do with the active voice. There seems to be a fairly general misapprehension of personal pronouns and voice in the literature of natural resource science. Referees and editors often state "use the active voice" when they mean "use personal pronouns." "We ate" is not in the active voice, despite the personal pronoun, because the verb (*ate*) is intransitive in this case (carries no action to the object of the sentence because there is no object). Use of personal pronouns is a matter of style at technical journals nowadays. These pronouns supplanted awkward constructs such as "the author" instead of "I" and rampant application of the passive voice in earlier technical writing. The use of personal pronouns was viewed as untidily subjective by early scientific writers. (Note that the preceding sentence is in the passive voice because I wanted "use," not "writers," to be more prominent as the subject of the sentence.)

There are some guidelines on making your paper comprehensible to readers, including referees and editors. In general, shorter words are more communicative than longer words. (By "communicative," I mean "transmits information in the most comprehensible manner.") If 2 words are synonyms, the shorter might be preferable to the longer. However, words carry shades of meaning (connotations), and in the interest of accuracy of message, you might apply the longer word. Referees and editors have access to dictionaries. Also, shorter sentences are more communicative than longer sentences, and shorter paragraphs are more communicative than longer paragraphs. So you have the option of breaking longer sentences or paragraphs into parts to increase the comprehensibility of your manuscript.

Technical writing need not lack grace, though it usually does. Let me give you an example of technical writing with grace (Calder 2004:59).

> Poetic appeal evokes emotional support for nature conservation, but, for the actual implementation of conservation, nature must be approached with scientific understanding of the functional linkages between plants, animals, and their physical environment. Ralph Waldo Emerson's . . . insight was [most] appropriate: "Beyond their sensuous delight, the forms and colors of nature have a new charm for us in our perception, that not one ornament was added for ornament, but is a sign of some better health, or more excellent action."
>
> A fine example of such excellent action is pollination, a crucial linkage in most ecosystems.

You would not necessarily have to be a biologist to find these words inspiring and arousing. Calder wrote them to set up a review of migration and pollination by hummingbirds.

Grace is a matter of aesthetics. Calder starts with "poetic appeal," drops the name Ralph Waldo Emerson, and uses an Emerson quote. Direct quotes add human interest to writing. He uses the paragraph hook, "excellent action," for a seamless transition from the first to the second paragraph. Another property of graceful writing is variability in cadence associated with variability in sentence and paragraph length. Graceful writers use similes and metaphors: "Like the Kaibab deer herd, progress in wildlife science may be headed for a crash under the weight of unreliable knowledge" (Romesburg 1981:293). He likens, metaphorically, the potential crash of knowledge in wildlife science to the collapse of the Kaibab deer herd.

Repetitiveness is the antithesis of grace in writing. The best example you see nowadays is overuse of the personal pronouns *I* and *we* in technical writing. We studied . . . we measured . . . we counted . . . we weighed . . . we analyzed . . . we . . . we . . . we . . . This type of writing is stilted (artificially formal), and it "sounds" bad to your mind. You would not speak this way. You can eliminate the effect by restructuring the sentence or occasionally applying the passive voice. For example, "We estimated density with line transects" could be cast as "Line transects provided estimates of density;" both of these sentences are in the active voice. Alternatively, "Density was estimated with line transects" is in the passive voice. The sentences in quotes range from 35 to 39 characters, so there is not much gain in either brevity or prolixity with any of them.

In a tongue-in-cheek paper titled "How to Write Consistently Boring Scientific Literature," Sand-Jensen (2007) offered these guidelines for increasing the boredom of readers, which is similar to eliminating grace from papers:

> Avoid focus. Ramble about on side issues or even unrelated ones rather than getting to some point, such as a clear statement of hypothesis.
>
> Avoid originality. "Publications reporting experiments and observations that have been made 100 times before are really mind-numbing" (p. 724).
>
> Write long papers.
>
> Remove most implications and every speculation.
>
> Omit necessary steps of reasoning.
>
> Use many abbreviations and technical terms.

Degrade species and biology to statistical elements.

Quote numerous papers for self-evident statements.

I do not know the degree to which grace in your writing will increase the probability of acceptance for your manuscript, *given that you have publishable data*. I doubt whether most referees and editors would consciously recognize grace in a manuscript. However, I do think they would have the implicit feeling that they had just read a good paper, and, other conditions being equal, this would move them toward a positive recommendation on acceptance.

I conclude this section with 2 recommendations on how to assay your paper for grace and cogency. First, let the paper cool off by placing it out of your mind for some period (2 weeks works for me). Try to focus your mind on other issues. After this rest, you will be better able to see flaws. Second, read the paper out loud. This will help you find repetitiveness, cumbersome constructions, and other problems.

Submission and Fate

Before you submit an article to a journal, have 3–5 of your colleagues review it. Try to select reviewers who are experienced publishers as well as good and complete critics. Local review can identify flaws in a manuscript that, upon correction, will increase the probability of acceptance.

Submission

Submission of a manuscript is a fairly mechanical process. Nowadays, submissions are electronic at many journals. You will be asked to include a letter of transmittal, which states the manuscript is under exclusive consideration by the journal. It is unethical and inconsiderate to submit the same manuscript to different journals at the same time. The letter of transmittal is also a place to recommend referees for the paper. This recommendation is not necessary.

Revision

If referees and editors judge that your manuscript is or may be publishable, an editor will offer you the opportunity to revise the paper. Editorial comments might include some general observations as well as an enumerated list of known or perceived problems. The editor might identify problems he or she thinks are salient and in definite need of your attention.

The easiest way to revise is to make the recommended changes, but do not make changes that invoke incorrect meaning in your text. Rather, consider whether there is some problem in your writing such that you can accommodate the changes by rewriting the text. If not, you can rebut recommendations by explaining why you prefer the original wording.

If you are like me, you will find, in most cases, that you can accommodate nearly all of the recommendations. Then in your reply to the editor, you can point this out and list the few exceptions and why you considered them exceptions. Referees make plenty of mistakes, and these you will want to tactfully rebut.

I warn you that the peer-review process can be infuriating. Most referees are dispassionate and objective, but you get occasional yahoos who like to argue with exclamation points. These Philistines seem to think that a request to review a paper makes them omnipotent. Another thing that incenses me is referees arguing on the basis of human values rather than technical merit. The point I want to leave you with is that composure may be requisite in the revision process.

Rejection

What does rejection imply? It might imply that you do not have publishable results. Flaws in experimental design, the application of inappropriate methodology, and small sample sizes might generally lead to rejection. Perhaps the study was not particularly original and addressed a topic well understood and broadly published. Referees might see no sense in publishing further information on the topic. Upon rejection, you might want to reflect (in the purest sense of this word) on the merits of your paper relative to the concerns expressed by referees and editors. You might, accordingly, conclude that your best response is to let the paper die.

On the other hand, rejection might not necessarily imply that your results are unpublishable. It might imply that the referees and editors made a faulty decision on your paper. If you believe this, you might be tempted to appeal the decision with written counterarguments and explanations. In my opinion, there is not much sense in appealing a rejection. In my experience as an editor and an author, I have never seen a successful appeal, but it would be induction most indecent to suppose appeals always fail.

Rejection might imply that whereas the information presented was publishable, it was inappropriately packaged. By this I mean there might have been problems with style, writing, organization, interpretation, completeness of the presentation, methodology, and so on. Oftentimes, referees encounter apparently worthy results that are so poorly packaged that it is not worth their *time* to go into great detail on how to get a paper in shape for publication; editors' *time* commitments also play a role here. The editor may state in the rejection letter that there is *possibly* publishable information in a manuscript.

If you conclude your paper is meritorious, despite rejection, then you have 2 options. One is to revise and resubmit to the same outlet; perhaps the editor has even suggested this. Of course, you have that option independent of what the editor says. I once had a paper rejected, and I waited until a change of editorial staff and resubmitted to the same outlet. The paper was successful on the second try. It also was improved by comments of the original referees and editor.

Another option is to revise according to referee comments, change style and slant (as necessary), and submit to a different outlet. This is why I recommended having 3 outlets in mind in the initial stage of manuscript preparation.

Perspectives

In this chapter, I gave an overview of the publishing process and tips on increasing the odds that your submission will be accepted. I did not explicitly mention that your expertise as a grammarian and the depth of your knowledge on writing and composition are crucial adjuncts to the publishing process. I have found two books to be particularly helpful in these respects. *The Little, Brown Handbook* (Fowler 1986) provides detailed and comprehensive instruction on writing and using the tools of the English language such as punctuation marks. *Elements of Style* (Strunk and White 2000) is a classic, easy-to-read book on effective writing. Of course, style manuals for journals supersede information or guidelines obtained from other sources.

Epilogue

[T]here is more faith involved in science than many scientists would be prepared to admit.
—Brian L. Silver (1998:xvi)

[M]any people choose scientific beliefs the same way they choose to be Methodists, or Democrats, or Chicago Cubs fans. They judge science by how well it agrees with the way they want the world to be.
—Robert Park (2000:ix)

Thought can more easily traverse an unexplored region than it can undo what has been so thoroughly done as to be ingrained in unconscious habit.
—John Dewey (1910:121)

More than 20 years have elapsed since a teaching assignment piqued my interest in the nature of science, especially natural resource science. In the interim I have read stacks of books on the topic and walked hundreds of miles thinking about the nature of natural resource science. I have also had the practical experience of doing or directing scores of studies, the results of which are part of the permanent record. This study, thought, and experience, as embodied in the contents of this book, lead me to offer a few summary observations for the beginning scientist.

First, there are very few individual ideas that apply without dilemma across all of science, and this includes ideas thought to be sacrosanct. There is no single scientific method; there are many. Ockham's Razor is a guideline, not an omnibus canon of science. An untestable hypothesis may be worthy of scientific discussion. The H-D method is a way to do science, not *the* way; indeed, inductive science and deductive science are interdependent, for induction leads to ideas to test by deduction. Experimental science has a place in natural resource science, and so does observational science. The nature of the problem under study dictates which approach will be most appropriate. And do not forget that pure thought has added immensely to our understanding of nature, and this occurs outside both experimental and observational science.

Second, science is tribal and therefore ritualistic. The cultural beliefs of the scientific community enjoin the behavior (rituals) of its members. The recent enthrallment with model selection among wildlife scientists illustrates the negative effects of ritualism. Model selection papers seem to get accepted on the basis of adherence to protocol, for often they contain no useful information, or even asinine information. To forestall such outcomes, young scientists need to maintain a certain aloofness in their personal practice of science. They need to think more deeply about results than mere adherence to protocol entails. They need to ponder whether results bear any meaning.

Third, there are *no* approaches to science that free scientists from the need for human judgment on the results of studies. The so-called canons of science do not necessarily help. Statistical tests and best models provide evidence about ideas, not confirmation or disconfirmation of them. That evidence will be contingent upon nonevidential factors such as sample size and an arbitrary *P*-value. In the final analysis, no field study, except possibly a purely descriptive one, takes place without the imposition of before-the-study judgment. "It is often said that experiments should be made without preconceived ideas. That is impossible" (Henri Poincaré [1854–1919]; cited in Silver 1998:82–83). This condition in and of itself would seem to entail after-the-study judgment.

At this point you might be feeling insecure because there are few, if any, maxims that generalize over the practice of science. As a scientist, do not expect help from immutable laws of conduct; you are largely on your own.

But a corollary of that insecurity is freedom of mind. You are free to contemplate canons, maxims, and *shoulds* and to apply them where appropriate and to ignore them where not appropriate. You are free to enter the world of ideas, your thinking not fettered by the tribal aphorisms of your peers. There is nothing in science quite like unfettered thought.

Literature Cited

Abbott, E. A. 1992. Flatland: a romance in many dimensions. Dover Publications, Mineola, New York.

Adler, M. J. 1981. Six great ideas. Touchstone, New York, New York.

Alexander, R. M. 1996. Optima for animals. Princeton University Press, Princeton, New Jersey.

Anderson, D. R., K. P. Burnham, W. R. Gould, and S. Cherry. 2001. Concerns about finding effects that are actually spurious. Wildlife Society Bulletin 29:311–16.

Anderson, D. R., K. P. Burnham, and W. L. Thompson. 2000. Null hypothesis testing: problems, prevalence, and an alternative. Journal of Wildlife Management 64:912–23.

Anderson, J. A. 1995. An introduction to neural networks. MIT Press, Cambridge, Massachusetts.

Atkins, P. W. 1995. The limitless power of science. Pages 122–32 in J. Cornwell, editor. Nature's imagination. Oxford University Press, Oxford, United Kingdom.

Avise, J. C. 1994. Molecular markers, natural history and evolution. Chapman & Hall, New York, New York.

Bakan, D. 1970. The test of significance in psychological research. Pages 231–51 in D. E. Morrison and R. E. Henkel, editors. The significance test controversy. Aldine Publishing Company, Chicago, Illinois.

Bandyopadhyay, P. S., and J. G. Bennett. 2004. Commentary. Pages 32–39 in Mark L. Taper and Subhash R. Lele, editors. The nature of scientific evidence. University of Chicago Press, Chicago, Illinois.

Barrow, J. D. 1995. Theories of everything. Pages 45–63 in J. Cornwell, editor. Nature's imagination. Oxford University Press, Oxford, United Kingdom.

———. 1998. Impossibility: the limits of science and the science of limits. Oxford University Press, Oxford, United Kingdom.

Barten, N. L., R. T. Bowyer, and K. J. Jenkins. 2001. Habitat use by female caribou: tradeoffs associated with parturition. Journal of Wildlife Management 65:77–92.

Baumgartner, F. M. 1944. Bobwhite quail populations on hunted vs. protected areas. Journal of Wildlife Management 8:259–60.

Bellrose, F. C. 1976. Ducks, geese & swans of North America. Stackpole Books, Harrisburg, Pennsylvania.

Berman, M. 2000. The twilight of American culture. W. W. Norton, New York, New York.

Berns, G. S., J. Chappelow, C. F. Zink, G. Pagnoni, M. E. Martin-Skurski, and

J. Richards. 2005. Neurobiological correlates of social conformity and independence during mental rotation. Biological Psychiatry 58:245–53.

Beveridge, W. I. B. 1957. The art of scientific investigation. Vintage Books, New York, New York.

Blackmore, S. 1999. The meme machine. Oxford University Press, Oxford, United Kingdom.

Bolger, D. T., M. A. Patten, and D. C. Bostock. 2005. Avian reproductive failure in response to an extreme climatic event. Oecologia 142:398–406.

Braun, C. E., editor. 2005. Techniques for wildlife investigations and management. The Wildlife Society, Bethesda, Maryland.

Bronowski, J. 1965. Science and human values. Harper & Row, New York, New York.

———. 1973. The ascent of man. Little, Brown, Boston, Massachusetts.

Brothers, L. 1997. Friday's footprint: how society shapes the human mind. Oxford University Press, New York, New York.

Brown, H. I. 2000. Judgment, role in science. Pages 194–202 *in* W. H. Newton-Smith, editor. A companion to the philosophy of science. Blackwell Publishers, Malden, Massachusetts.

Brown, J. H. 2000. Thought experiments. Pages 528–31 *in* W. H. Newton-Smith, editor. A companion to the philosophy of science. Blackwell Publishers, Malden, Massachusetts.

Buckland, S. T., D. R. Anderson, K. P. Burnham, and J. L. Laake. 1993. Distance sampling. Chapman & Hall, London, United Kingdom.

Buehler, D. A., T. J. Mersmann, J. D. Fraser, and J. K. D. Seegar. 1991. Nonbreeding bald eagle communal and solitary roosting behavior and roost habitat on the northern Chesapeake Bay. Journal of Wildlife Management 55:273–81.

Burger, L. W., Jr., M. R. Ryan, T. V. Dailey, and E. W. Kurzejeski. 1995. Reproductive strategies, success, and mating systems of northern bobwhite in Missouri. Journal of Wildlife Management 59:417–26.

Burnham, K. P., and D. R. Anderson. 1998. Model selection and inference. Springer, New York, New York.

———. 2002. Model selection and multimodel inference. Springer-Verlag, New York, New York.

Burnham, K. P., D. R. Anderson, and J. L. Laake. 1980. Estimation of density from line transect sampling of biological populations. Wildlife Monographs 72:1–202.

Calder, W. A. 2004. Rufous and broad-tailed hummingbirds. Pages 59–79 *in* G. P. Nabhan, editor. Conserving migratory pollinators and nectar corridors in western North America. University of Arizona Press, Tucson, Arizona.

Campbell, S. K. 1974. Flaws and fallacies in statistical thinking. Prentice-Hall, Englewood Cliffs, New Jersey.

Case, R. M. 1972. Energetic requirements for egg-laying bobwhites. Proceedings of the National Bobwhite Quail Symposium 1:205–12.

Chamberlin, T. C. 1890. The method of multiple working hypotheses. Science 15:92.

Cherry, S. 1998. Statistical tests in publications of the Wildlife Society. Wildlife Society Bulletin 26:947–53.

Cohen, J., and I. Stewart. 1994. The collapse of chaos—discovering simplicity in a complex world. Penguin Books, New York, New York.

Conner, L. M. 2001. Survival and cause-specific mortality of adult fox squirrels in southwestern Georgia. Journal of Wildlife Management 65:200–204.

Cornaglia, P. S., G. E. Schrant, M. Nardi, and V. E. Deregibus. 2005. Emergence of Dallisgrass as affected by soil water availability. Rangeland Ecology & Management 58:35–40.

Cox, S. A., F. S. Guthery, J. J. Lusk, A. D. Peoples, S. J. DeMaso, and M. Sams. 2005. Reproduction by bobwhites in western Oklahoma. Journal of Wildlife Management 69:133–39.

Curtis, P. D., and P. G. Jensen. 2004. Habitat features affecting beaver occupancy along roadsides in New York State. Journal of Wildlife Management 68:278–87.

Curtis, P. D., B. S. Mueller, P. D. Doerr, C. F. Robinette, and T. DeVos. 1993. Potential polygamous breeding behavior in northern bobwhite. Proceedings of the National Quail Symposium 3:55–63.

Darwin, C. R. 1859. On the origin of species by means of natural selection. John Murray, London, United Kingdom.

Davison, V. E. 1949. Bobwhites on the rise. Charles Scribner's Sons, New York, New York.

Dawkins, R. 1976. The selfish gene. Oxford University Press, Oxford, United Kingdom.

Delehanty, D. J., S. S. Eaton, and T. G. Campbell. 2004. Mountain quail fidelity to guzzlers in the Mojave Desert. Wildlife Society Bulletin 32:588–93.

DeVos, T., and B. S. Mueller. 1993. Reproductive ecology of northern bobwhite in north Florida. Proceedings of the National Quail Symposium 3:83–90.

Dewey, J. 1910. How we think. D. C. Heath, Boston, Massachusetts.

Diamond, J. 1997. Guns, germs, and steel—the fate of human societies. W. W. Norton, New York, New York.

Eberhardt, L. L. 1970. Correlation, regression, and density dependence. Ecology 51:306–10.

Eddington, Sir A. S. 2000. The constants of nature. Pages 1075–93 *in* J. Newman, editor. The world of mathematics. Volume 2. Dover Publications, Mineola, New York.

Edmonds, D., and J. Eidinow. 2001. Wittgenstein's poker. HarperCollins, New York, New York.

Edwards, A. W. F. 1992. Likelihood. Johns Hopkins University Press, Baltimore, Maryland.

Eigen, M., and R. Winkler 1981. The laws of the game. Princeton University Press, Princeton, New Jersey.

Einstein, A. 1961. Relativity. Wings Books, New York, New York.

Ellis, J. A., K. P. Thomas, and P. Moore. 1972. Bobwhite whistling activity and population density on two public hunting areas in Illinois. Proceedings of the National Bobwhite Quail Symposium 1:282–88.

Errington, P. L. 1945. Some contributions of a fifteen-year local study of the northern bobwhite to a knowledge of population phenomena. Ecological Monographs 15:1–34.

Errington, P. L., and F. N. Hammerstrom Jr. 1935. Bob-white winter survival on experimentally shot and unshot areas. Iowa State College Journal of Science 9:625–39.

Feynman, R. P. 1998. The meaning of it all. Perseus Books, Reading, Massachusetts.

Flint, P. L. 1998. Settlement rate of lead shot in tundra wetlands. Journal of Wildlife Management 62:1099–1102.

Fowler, H. R. 1986. The Little, Brown handbook. Little, Brown, Boston, Massachusetts.

Fries, J. F. 1984. The compression of morbidity: miscellaneous comments about a theme. Gerontologist 24:354–59.

Garton, E. O., J. T. Ratti, and J. H. Giudice. 2005. Research and experimental design. Pages 43–71 *in* C. E. Braun, editor. Techniques for wildlife investigations and management. The Wildlife Society, Bethesda, Maryland.

Giles, R. H., Jr. 1978. Wildlife management. W. H. Freeman, San Francisco, California.

Glading, B., and R. W. Saarni. 1944. Effect of hunting on a valley quail population. California Fish and Game 30:71–79.

Gould, S. J. 1993. Eight little piggies: reflections in natural history. W. W. Norton, New York, New York.

Grandin, T., and C. Johnson. 2004. Animals in translation. Scribner, New York, New York.

Gross, P. R., and N. Levitt. 1994. Higher superstition—the academic left and its quarrels with science. Johns Hopkins University Press, Baltimore, Maryland.

Guthery, F. S. 1997. A philosophy of habitat management for northern bobwhites. Journal of Wildlife Management 61:291–301.

———. 1999a. The role of free water in bobwhite management. Wildlife Society Bulletin 27:538–42.

———. 1999b. Slack in the configuration of habitat patches for northern bobwhites. Journal of Wildlife Management 63:245–50.

———. 2000. On bobwhites. Texas A&M University Press, College Station, Texas.

———. 2002. The technology of bobwhite management: the theory behind the practice. Iowa State University Press, Ames, Iowa.

———. 2004. Commentary: the flavors and colors of facts in wildlife science. Wildlife Society Bulletin 32:288–97.

Guthery, F. S., and R. L. Bingham. 1992. On Leopold's principle of edge. Wildlife Society Bulletin 20:340–44.

———. 1996. A theoretical basis for study and management of trampling by cattle. Journal of Range Management 49:264–69.

Guthery, F. S., L. A. Brennan, M. J. Peterson, and J. J. Lusk. 2005. Information theory in wildlife science: critique and viewpoint. Journal of Wildlife Management 69:457–65.

Guthery, F. S., M. C. Green, R. E. Masters, S. J. DeMaso, H. M. Wilson, and F. B. Steubing. 2001. Land cover and bobwhite abundance on Oklahoma farms and ranches. Journal of Wildlife Management 65:838–49.

Guthery, F. S., N. M. King, K. R. Nolte, W. P. Kuvlesky Jr., S. DeStefano, S. A. Gall, and N. J. Silvy. 2001. Multivariate perspectives on patch use by masked bobwhites. Journal of Wildlife Management 65:118–24.

Guthery, F. S., and W. P. Kuvlesky Jr. 1998. The effect of multiple-brooding on age ratios of quail. Journal of Wildlife Management 62:540–49.

Guthery, F. S., C. L. Land, and B. W. Hall. 2001. Heat loads on reproducing bobwhites in the semiarid subtropics. Journal of Wildlife Management 65:111–17.

Guthery, F. S., J. J. Lusk, and M. J. Peterson. 2001. The fall of the null hypothesis: liabilities and opportunities. Journal of Wildlife Management 65:379–84.

———. 2004. Hypotheses in wildlife science. Wildlife Society Bulletin 32:1325–32.

Guthery, F. S., M. J. Peterson, and R. R. George. 2000. Viability of northern bobwhite populations. Journal of Wildlife Management 64:646–62.

Guthery, F. S., M. J. Peterson, J. L. Lusk, M. J. Rabe, S. J. DeMaso, M. Sams, R. D. Applegate, and T. V. Dailey. 2004. Multi-state analysis of fixed, liberal regulations in quail harvest management. Journal of Wildlife Management 68:1104–13.

Guthery, F. S., A. R. Rybak, S. D. Fuhlendorf, T. L. Hiller, S. G. Smith,

W. H. Puckett Jr., and R. A. Baker. 2005. Aspects of the thermal ecology of bobwhites in north Texas. Wildlife Monographs 159:1–36.

Hagood, M. J. 1970. The notion of a hypothetical universe. Pages 65–78 *in* D. E. Morrison and R. E. Henkel, editors. The significance test controversy. Aldine Publishing Company, Chicago, Illinois.

Hale-Evans, R. 2006. Mind performance hacks. O'Reilly Media, Sebastopol, California.

Harris, S. 2005. The end of faith. W. W. Norton, New York, New York.

Hayne, D. W. 1949. Two methods for estimating populations from trapping records. Journal of Mammalogy 30:399–411.

Hawking, S. W. 1988. A brief history of time from the Big Bang to black holes. Bantam, Toronto, Canada.

Hilborn, R., and M. Mangel. 1997. The ecological detective. Princeton University Press, Princeton, New Jersey.

Hiller, T. L., and F. S. Guthery. 2004. Correlates of fall-spring mass dynamics of northern bobwhites. Wilson Bulletin 116:324–29.

———. 2005. Microclimate versus predation risk in roost and covert selection by bobwhites. Journal of Wildlife Management 69:140–49.

Houghton, J. 1994. Global warming—the complete briefing. Cambridge University Press, Cambridge, United Kingdom.

Howson, C. 2000. Induction and the uniformity of nature. Pages 181–83 *in* W. H. Newton-Smith, editor. A companion to the philosophy of science. Blackwell Publishers, Malden, Massachusetts.

Humphreys, P. 2000. Causation. Pages 31–40 *in* W. H. Newton-Smith, editor. Companion to the philosophy of science. Blackwell Publishers, Malden, Massachusetts.

Hurlbert, S. H. 1984. Pseudoreplication and the design of ecological field experiments. Ecological Monographs 54:187–211.

Hutchinson, G. E. 1957. Concluding remarks. Cold Spring Harbor Symposium on Quantitative Biology 22:415–27.

Jackson, V. L., L. L. Laack, and E. G. Zimmerman. 2005. Landscape metrics associated with habitat use by ocelots in South Texas. Journal of Wildlife Management 69:733–38.

Johnson, D. B., and F. S. Guthery. 1988. Loafing coverts used by northern bobwhites in subtropical environments. Journal of Wildlife Management 52:464–69.

Johnson, D. H. 1999. The insignificance of statistical significance testing. Journal of Wildlife Management 63:763–72.

———. 2002. The importance of replication in wildlife research. Journal of Wildlife Management 66:919–32.

Johnson, D. H., T. L. Shaffer, and W. E. Newton. 2001. Statistics for wildlifers: how much and what kind? Wildlife Society Bulletin 29:1055–60.

Johnson, J. B., and K. S. Omland. 2004. Model selection in ecology and evolution. Trends in Evolution and Ecology 19:101–26.

Kadane, J. B., and N. A. Lazar. 2004. Methods and criteria for model selection. Journal of the American Statistical Association 99:279–90.

Kaku, M. 1994. Hyperspace. Anchor Books, New York, New York.

Kaminer, W. 1999. Sleeping with extra-terrestrials. Pantheon Books, New York, New York.

Kaplan, R. 2000. The nothing that is: the natural history of zero. Oxford University Press, Oxford, United Kingdom.

Kasner, E., and J. R. Newman. 2000. New names for old. Pages 1996–2010 *in* J. Newman, editor. The world of mathematics. Volume 3. Dover Publications, Mineola, New York.

Kellert, S. H. 1993. In the wake of chaos: unpredictable order in dynamical systems. University of Chicago Press, Chicago, Illinois.

Kleinbaum, D. G. 1994. Logistic regression. Springer-Verlag, New York, New York.

Kosko, B. 1992. Neural networks and fuzzy systems. Prentice-Hall, Englewood Cliffs, New Jersey.

———. 1993. Fuzzy thinking. Hyperion, New York, New York.

Lack, D. 1954. The natural regulation of animal numbers. Oxford University Press, Oxford, United Kingdom.

Lambin, X. 1994. Natal philopatry, competition for resources, and inbreeding avoidance in Townsend's voles (*Microtus townsendii*). Ecology 74:224–35.

Larsen, K. W., and S. Boutin. 1994. Movements, survival, and settlement of red squirrel (*Tamiasciurus hudsonicus*) offspring. Ecology 75:214–23.

Leopold, A. 1933. Game management. Charles Scribner's Sons, New York, New York.

Little, T. W., and K. L. Varland. 1981. Reproduction and dispersal of transplanted wild turkeys in Iowa. Journal of Wildlife Management 45:419–27.

Lochmiller, R. L., M. R. Vesky, and S. T. McMurry. 1994. Temporal variation in humoral and cell-mediated immune response in a *Sigmodon hispidus* population. Ecology 75:236–45.

Loehle, C. 1990. A guide to increased creativity in research—inspiration or perspiration? BioScience 40:123–29.

Lopez, B. 2004. Of wolves and men. Scribner, New York, New York.

Lusk, J. J., F. S. Guthery, S. A. Cox, S. J. DeMaso, and A. D. Peoples. 2005. Survival and growth of northern bobwhite chicks in western Oklahoma. American Midland Naturalist 153:389–95.

Lyon, L. A., and D. F. Caccamise. 1981. Habitat selection by roosting blackbirds and starlings: management implications. Journal of Wildlife Management 45:435–43.

McNeill, W. H. 1998. Plagues and peoples. Anchor Books, New York, New York.

Mandelbrot, B. B. 1983. The fractal geometry of nature. W. H. Freeman, New York, New York.

March, J. G. 1994. A primer on decision making: how decisions happen. Free Press, New York, New York.

Mayfield, H. 1961. Nesting success calculated from exposure. Wilson Bulletin 73:255–61.

Meine, C. 1988. Aldo Leopold: his life and work. University of Wisconsin Press, Madison, Wisconsin.

Merrill, E. H., J. J. Hartigan, and M. W. Meyer. 2005. Does prey biomass or mercury exposure affect loon chick survival in Wisconsin? Journal of Wildlife Management 69:57–67.

Moroney, M. J. 2000. On the average and scatter. Pages 1487–1511 *in* J. Newman, editor. The world of mathematics. Volume 3. Dover Publications, Mineola, New York.

Morrison, D. E., and R. E. Henkel, editors. 1970. The significance test controversy. Aldine, Chicago, Illinois.

Morrison, M. L. 2005. Viewpoints, genetics, and free lunch. Journal of Wildlife Management 69:1313–14.

Mosby, H. S. 1963. Wildlife investigational techniques. The Wildlife Society, Bethesda, Maryland.

Newton-Smith, W. H. 2000. Hume. Pages 165–68 *in* W. H. Newton-Smith, editor. A companion to the philosophy of science. Blackwell Publishers, Malden, Massachusetts.

O'Keefe, J. H., and L. Cordain. 2004. Cardiovascular disease resulting from a diet and lifestyle at odds with our Paleolithic genome: how to become a 21st-century hunter-gatherer. Mayo Clinic Proceedings 79:101–108.

Oreskes, N., K. Shrader-Frechette, and K. Belitz. 1994. Verification, validation, and confirmation of numerical models in the earth sciences. Science 263:641–46.

Palahniuk, C. 2001. Choke. Anchor Books, New York, New York.

Park, R. 2000. Voodoo science. Oxford University Press, Oxford, United Kingdom.

Parmalee, P. W. 1953. Hunting pressure and its effect on bobwhite quail populations in east-central Texas. Journal of Wildlife Management 17:341–45.

Patten, M. A., D. H. Wolfe, E. Shochat, and S. K. Sherrod. 2005. Effects of microhabitat and microclimate selection on adult survivorship of the lesser prairie-chicken. Journal of Wildlife Management 69:1270–78.

Patterson, B. R., and F. Messier. 2000. Factors influencing killing rates of white-tailed deer by coyotes in eastern Canada. Journal of Wildlife Management 64:721–32.

Pechacek, P., and A. Kristin. 2004. Comparative diets of adult and young three-toed woodpeckers in a European alpine forest community. Journal of Wildlife Management 68:683–93.

Peirce, C. S. 2000. The probability of induction. Pages 1341–54 *in* J. Newman, editor. The world of mathematics. Volume 2. Dover Publications, Mineola, New York.

Peters, T. J., and R. H. Waterman Jr. 1982. In search of excellence. Warner Books, New York, New York.

Peterson, T. L., and J. A. Cooper. 1987. Impacts of center pivot irrigation systems on birds in prairie wetlands. Journal of Wildlife Management 51:238–47.

Pinker, S. 1997. How the mind works. W. W. Norton, New York, New York.

Plotkin, H. 2000. Culture and psychological mechanisms. Pages 69–82 *in* R. Aunger, editor. Darwinizing culture. Oxford University Press, Oxford, United Kingdom.

Poincaré, H. 1952. Science and hypothesis. Dover Publications, New York, New York.

———. 2000. Mathematical creation. Pages 2041–50 *in* Jo Newman, editor. The world of mathematics, Volume 4. Dover Publications, Mineola, New York.

Popper, K. R. 1959. The logic of scientific discovery. Basic Books, New York, New York.

Radomski, A. A., and F. S. Guthery. 2000. Theory of the hunter-covey interface. Proceedings of the National Quail Symposium 4:78–81.

Rave, D. P., and G. A. Baldassarre. 1991. Carcass mass and composition of green-winged teal wintering in Louisiana and Texas. Journal of Wildlife Management 55: 457–61.

Robbins, T. 2000. Fierce invalids home from hot climates. Bantam Books, New York, New York.

Rolstad, J., E. Rolstad, and Ø. Saeteven. 2000. Black woodpecker nest sites: characteristics, selection, and reproductive success. Journal of Wildlife Management 64:1053–66.

Romesburg, H. C. 1981. Wildlife science: gaining reliable knowledge. Journal of Wildlife Management 45:293–313.

———. 1991. On improving the natural resources and environmental sciences. Journal of Wildlife Management 55:744–56.

Rosch, E. 1975. Cognitive representations of semantic categories. Journal of Experimental Psychology: General 104:192–233.

Rosen, R. 1991. Life itself: a comprehensive inquiry into the nature, origin, and fabrication of life. Columbia University Press, Columbia, New York.

Rosenberg, D. K., and R. G. Anthony. 1993. Differences in Townsend's chipmunk populations between second- and old-growth forests in western Oregon. Journal of Wildlife Management 57:365–73.

Rozeboom, W. W. 1970. The fallacy of the null hypothesis significance test. Pages 216–30 *in* D. E. Morrison and R. E. Henkel, editors. The significance test controversy. Aldine, Chicago, Illinois.

Russell, B. 2000. Mathematics and the metaphysicians. Pages 1576–90 *in* J. Newman, editor. The world of mathematics. Volume 3. Dover Publications, Mineola, New York.

Sackett, D. L., S. E. Stratus, W. S. Richardson, W. Rosenberg, and R. B. Haynes. 2000. Evidence-based medicine. Churchill Livingston, New York, New York.

Sagan, C. 1997. Billions & billions. Random House, New York, New York.

Sand-Jensen, K. 2007. How to write consistently boring scientific literature. Oikos 116:723–27.

Schmidly, D. J. 2005. What it means to be a naturalist and the future of natural history at American universities. Journal of Mammalogy 86:449–56.

Schwartz, C. C., and K. J. Hundertmark. 1993. Reproductive characteristics of Alaskan moose. Journal of Wildlife Management 57:454–66.

Seager, W. 2000. Metaphysics, role in science. Pages 283–92 *in* W. H. Newton-Smith, editor. A companion to the philosophy of science. Blackwell Publishers, Malden, Massachusetts.

Sermons, W. O., and D. W. Speake. 1987. Production of second broods by bobwhites. Wilson Bulletin 99:285–86.

Shafer, C. L. 1990. Nature preserves. Smithsonian Institution Press, Washington, D.C.

Silver, B. L. 1998. The ascent of science. Oxford University Press, Oxford, United Kingdom.

Sinclair, A. R. E. 1991. Science and the practice of wildlife management. Journal of Wildlife Management 55:767–73.

Skrabanek, P. 2000. False premises, false promises. Skrabanek Foundation, Dublin, Ireland.

Smith, L. M., J. W. Hupp, and J. T. Ratti. 1982. Habitat use and home range of gray partridge in eastern South Dakota. Journal of Wildlife Management 46:580–87.

Smith, M. 1996. Neural networks for statistical modeling. International Thomson Computer Press, London, United Kingdom.

Smith, N. S. 1988. Predictable results and peer review. Wildlife Society Bulletin 16:225–26.

Sorenson, R. A. 1992. Thought experiments. Oxford University Press, New York, New York.

Spears, G. S., F. S. Guthery, S. M. Rice, S. J. DeMaso, and B. Zaiglin. 1993. Optimum seral stage for bobwhites as influenced by site productivity. Journal of Wildlife Management 57:805–11.

Stanford, J. A. 1972. Bobwhite quail population dynamics: relationships of weather, nesting, production patterns, fall population characteristics, and harvest in Missouri quail. Proceedings of the National Bobwhite Quail Symposium 1:115–39.

Steinbeck, J. 1994. The short reign of Pippin IV. Penguin Books, New York, New York.

Stephens, P. A., S. W. Buskirk, and C. M. del Rio. 2006. Inference in ecology and evolution. Trends in Ecology and Evolution 22:192–97.

Stephens, P. A., S. W. Buskirk, G. D. Hayward, and C. Martinez del Rio. 2005. Information theory and hypothesis testing: a call for pluralism. Journal of Applied Ecology 42:4–12.

Stewart, K. M., T. E. Fulbright, and D. L. Drawe. 2000. White-tailed deer use of clearings relative to forage availability. Journal of Wildlife Management 64:733–41.

Stoddard, H. L. 1931. The bobwhite quail: its habits, preservation and increase. Charles Scribner's Sons, New York, New York.

Strickland, B. K., and S. Demarais. 2000. Age and regional differences in antlers and mass of white-tailed deer. Journal of Wildlife Management 64:903–11.

Strogatz, S. H. 1994. Nonlinear dynamics and chaos. Addison-Wesley, Reading, Massachusetts.

Strunk, W., Jr., and E. B. White. 2000. The elements of style. Longman, New York, New York.

Suchy, W. J., and R. J. Munkel 1993. Breeding strategies of the northern bobwhite in marginal habitat. Proceedings of the National Quail Symposium 3:69–78.

Talent, L. G., G. L. Krapu, and R. L. Jarvis. 1982. Habitat use by mallard broods in south central North Dakota. Journal of Wildlife Management 46:629–35.

Taylor, J. S. 1991. Aspects of northern bobwhite reproductive biology in South Texas. Master's thesis, Texas A&I University, Kingsville, Texas.

Thompson, D. R., and C. Kabat. 1949. Hatching dates of quail in Wisconsin. Journal of Wildlife Management 13:231–33.

Thompson, T. W., B. A. Roundy, E. D. McArthur, B. D. Jessop, B. Waldron, and J. W. Davis. 2006. Fire rehabilitation using native and introduced species: a landscape trial. Rangeland Ecology & Management 59:237–48.

Vaughan, M. R., and L. B. Keith. 1981. Demographic response of experimental snowshoe hare populations to overwinter food shortage. Journal of Wildlife Management 45:354–80.

von Oech, R. 1990. A whack on the side of the head. Warner Books, New York, New York.

Vyse, S. A. 1997. Believing in magic: the psychology of superstition. Oxford University Press, New York, New York.

Werner, E. E. 1994. Ontogenetic scaling of competitive relations: size-dependent effects and responses in two anuran larvae. Ecology 75:197–213.

Weyl, H. 2000. The mathematical way of thinking. Pages 1823–49 *in* J. Newman, editor. The world of mathematics. Volume 3. Dover Publications, Mineola, New York.

Whitehead, A. N. 2000. Mathematics as an element in the history of thought. Pages 402–16 *in* J. Newman, editor. The world of mathematics. Volume 1. Dover, Mineola, New York.

Williams, J. E., and S. C. Kendeigh. 1982. Energetics of the Canada goose. Journal of Wildlife Management 46:588–600.

Wilson, E. O. 1998. Consilience: the unity of knowledge. Alfred A. Knopf, New York, New York.

Ziman, J. 1978. Reliable knowledge: an exploration of the grounds for belief in science. Cambridge University Press, Cambridge, United Kingdom.

Index

ISBN-13: 978-1-60344-024-0
ISBN-10: 1-60344-024-0